THE DIARY
OF
BUA GEOW

J.C. SHAW

A novel set in twentieth century Chiang Mai

Illustrations by Susie Hampshire

By the same author

Northern Thai Ceramics
Introducing Thai Ceramics
The Ramayana – through western eyes
The Seal of Tammatari
The Paston Papers

ISBN   974-7315-59–9

Printed in Thailand by Craftsman Press
Soi Watanasilp, Pratunam, Bangkok
Telephone 02-253009, 2533298

Bua Geow is a disabled village girl who lives, today, near Chiang Mai. She tells a simple tale of how she became paralysed after jumping from a brothel window, of the daily life and problems of her family and how she finally finds happiness.

She talks, too, of her bewitchingly beautiful friend, whom we called Tari, but whose full name was Tammatari. The future Miss Thailand and, could it be, the past Princess?

Preface to the Second Edition

The Diary of Bua Geow was originally published in 1985 as Part II of **The Seal of Tammatari.**

Here it is published on its own – she has added some new remarks on electricity and on land development. She has also added notes, not by her, on Buddhism, ceramics and a gossip column article on Tari.

Part I of **The Seal of Tammatari, The Paston Papers,** has also been reissued as a separate book.

> There are those who think that there is a
> connection between the two books

Dedication

เพื่อคนไทยทุกคน

I never knew Bua Geow had followed my casual suggestion that she should keep a diary to help pass the time until, one day, she shyly handed me a rather grubby school exercise book with the command that it should not be opened until I reached home.

That evening, as I slowly turned the pages, I realised that this was not so much a diary, for the passage of days had but little meaning for her, but more reflections on her village, the people and their ways and their thoughts, on the countryside, the seasons and the harvests, on her own beliefs and feelings – a scrapbook, perhaps.

When finally I laid the book aside, Bua Geow's soft northern Thai voice continued speaking clearly in my mind, sad with suffering yet lilting with hope and joy. She seemed somehow, in her complete simplicity, to speak for all the silent country girls of Thailand.

I knew then that she would go on writing her diary and that it would be my duty to translate it and to have it published, difficult though this would be. Difficult because she writes often of my wife and myself and also because my Thai is not fluent.

I have tried to stay as close as possible to her original words, but where the Thai does not translate comfortably into English I have made some small alterations whilst, as far as possible, retaining the original meaning. I have not translated proper names as, so often, they sound ridiculous. Bua Geow tends to jump backwards and forwards in time and from subject to subject, sometimes returning to a matter I thought had been forgotten. I have not attempted to change her style but have indicated a break where the jumps are most dramatic.

The rains came late this year and father had been worrying that the rice would suffer but, for the past three days, it has rained without cease; I have not once been able to go outside and the mountains have been quite hidden. The River is as full as I have ever seen it. I should explain that our house is within whispering distance of the River Ping, luckily the bank here is high and it has never flooded. The swollen waters are only a few feet from the top as they sweep silently and sullenly past, bearing rafts of water-hyacinth, straw or tree trunks, on which I sometimes see little frightened animals or a waving snake. Further up the River, my brother tells me, twenty *rai* of garlic, planted only last week, have been washed away and the straw I see floating past must come from those fields, some of which belong to Daeng who, only last week, was saying how clever he had been to have planted early so that his crop would fetch a much higher price than father's.

The River is rich brown in colour, I suppose because of all the soil it has stolen from farmers like Daeng, soil that it will give back to others in the plains of the south. To me the River certainly has a spirit. It does good or evil, it is full and fat or starved and dry, cheerful or sad; just as our lives change, so does the River. It is good sometimes to pay our respects to its spirit although I doubt if this alters anything any more than we can change the course of our own lives – as I should know.

At least the River is fairly predictable. I know that next week the floods will have gone from here, moving first through the riverside streets and schools of Chiang Mai – I expect Pim will have a holiday as Regina College always floods – and then on to add to the misery of the Bangkok people. I know that in a few months' time my sister, Tip, will be planting *mun geow* and other vegetables in the dry and fertile river bed in front of our house and that she will,

4

as every year, have to cut new steps down the steep bank, a task that used to be mine.

This afternoon mother came to sit beside me, as always she spoke hardly a word but yet I feel her deep love and it comforts me. She is only just forty, but already an old woman, her face criss-crossed with deep lines, worn out by years of work, worry and poverty. In spite of everything she has kept her self-respect and her faith and she invariably looks tidy in her white blouse and her black *pasin*, fringed with stripes of red and gold.

I always remember her as looking old. Most of the girls I know look so, after they have married and had a few children, certainly by the time they are twenty-five. In the big towns I notice that people do not have the worn and wrinkled faces that we in the villages do. It must be the work in the fields or could it be, I wonder, that the food we eat is not good enough ? Sticky rice every, every day with often little but chillies, garlic and fish sauce to flavour it. The food I saw in Mae Khun's house was certainly very different, although I did not like it myself.

My brother, Chand, had a row with Uncle Put this morning. Chand refused to lend him our water-pump because last year he broke it and would not pay for it to be mended. I think Chand is too hard since Put has already planted two and a half *rai* of garlic and it will die if not watered. I know no one else will lend him a pump and I am sure he can not afford to buy one.

Yesterday I wrote my diary for the first time and I rather enjoyed it; I think it was a good idea of Por Khun's but I don't think I will write every day as so often so very little happens. I have bought seven yellow books like the ones I used to use at school. I wonder if I will fill even one, let alone seven! Today I will write a little about myself.

5

My name is Bua Geow and I live in the village of Mae Taeng, in the Province of Chiang Mai, in the north of Thailand. I was born in the second lunar month, that is to say, December, and I am nineteen years old. My parents can not remember the day on which I was born, nor did they register my birth, so I can not have a birthday party nor can I have my horoscope read; perhaps it does not matter. I live with my mother and father, elder brother, and two older sisters, one of whom is married with two children.

I will not write of my childhood as I can remember very little about it and what I do remember was not very interesting. What I write in the future will do very well to show what my life was like in the past. When I was seven I went to the *wat* school. Since this was in the next village it meant half an hour's walk, morning and evening; many children had much further to come. I enjoyed my six years at school, made many friends and luckily learned to read and write tolerably well.

During the long Songkram holiday in April which marks our New Year, although the real New Year when the first month begins is in November or December depending on the moon, and now, of course, the official New Year, which we also celebrate, is on January the First, during this holiday, Sak, who is a distant cousin, came to visit us from Bangkok. Sak was smartly dressed in tight fitting jeans held up by a leather belt with a large gold buckle, a bright blue shirt with a crocodile on it, pointed shiny shoes and long shiny hair.

He showed off his city superiority, laughing at his parents and the stupid villagers who lived such a poor and ignorant life. He very much impressed me and my best friend, Lynn. Lynn and I had planned to save up and each buy a sewing machine so that we could start a small business making clothes to sell in the village. We thought it would take us three years of hard work to make enough money. When we told our plans to Sak he roared with laughter and said that we could save the Bts 3,000 that we each wanted within three months in Bangkok. He had a friend who owned a restaurant and was looking for waitresses. We could live there free and the tips were good.

"In fact," he said, "my friend asked me to bring two pretty girls back with him. He even advanced the money to pay for their train fares."

We did not take much persuading and our parents readily agreed since Sak was a relative and clearly a sophisticated and prosperous one. We spent the last of our savings buying a few clothes and shoes that we thought would be suitable for Bangkok. We set gaily off in the mini-bus, our few possessions stuffed into plastic bags.

Chiang Mai Station, the end of the northern railway line, was bustling with passengers busy buying sticky rice and roast chicken or pork for the long night journey. In the evening sunlight, the train rolled noisily along the valley to Lampun, through the dried up rice fields and past the rich *lamyai* orchards, heavy with sweet smelling blossom. Doi Sutep was lost in the distance, and then began the slow climb up the mountains. We watched the girls, girls like us, leading home the buffaloes, watering the vegetables from two heavy cans suspended from a pole across their shoulders or washing themselves in the streams. Oh, how superior we felt riding by on our way to a grand life in Bangkok!

By the time we reached Kun Tan and the tunnel at the top of the pass it was nearly dark, and I remember that the little wild orchids, held up to the train windows by children, looked like small sticks of light. For the rest of the night journey we dozed on the wooden seats, pleasantly half awakened as the train jerked to a halt in Den Chai,

Pitsanuloke, Ayuthya or one of the other stations, at all of which were people selling coffee, sweets or sticky rice. *"Oliang! Kanom! Khao niew!"* they called as they walked past the windows. And so, on a hot April morning, we arrived at Hua Lampong, the station of Bangkok, or as it is called in Thai, Krung Tep, the City of Angels, the city of our hopes.

That night there were no angels to help Lynn and me. Nightmares that did not fade on waking. Bodies and pain, bodies and shame, that night. That night we were raped again and again by the men who worked in the brothel. I heard Lynn's cries in the next room through the thin partition and she must have heard mine. I do not want to write about it or about the days and nights that followed. Indeed, I remember it now in a detached way as if seen through a dirty window-pane in my mind. After all, it happened to another girl in another life.

There were fifteen girls mostly from the north and none over twenty years old. We were kept upstairs, locked in and never once allowed outside. All our clothes, the new ones we had chosen with such care, were taken away and all we were given to wear was a *pasin*. We all slept on the floor in one room and it was there that the guests came to choose one of us – often we had to bare our breasts for them to see – and take her away to one of the eight small bedrooms.

I do not remember the guests at all but, strangely, I did not feel disgust or anger against them even when they smelled of Mekong whisky or hurt me. I felt, I think, as a caged bird must feel. The day I arrived in Bangkok, youth and happiness were mine, the next day I was broken and empty. The brothel owner and his henchmen, the mamasan and above all my cousin Sak, these I could not forgive. They must have felt my hatred for I was always picked on to do the dirty chores and, although they did not dare to mark my body, they often used it.

One of the guest-rooms looked out over the street and because it was on the third floor, the window was not barred. If, I thought, a lorry happened to park under the window when I was tidying up after a guest had gone, maybe I could escape. It was the only way.

And so one evening I jumped.

Last night as I wrote, I stood again on the window-sill, but I could not bring myself to look down, nor can I now. So I will write first of other things, later, perhaps, I will be able to go on.

I have talked to girls who have had similar experiences, I have talked also to girls who worked of their own free-will in bars and massage parlours, and social workers have talked to me. To my mind the degradation came, not from the use of my body by the guests, but from the loss of my freedom and the cruelty of my captors. I think if they had used me for any other purpose it would have been equally humiliating. I am sure all innocent prisoners must feel the same. I can understand any girl who chooses to sell her body, for what else does a poor, uneducated village girl have to sell, and what is the alternative life like if she stays at home to become an old and worn- out woman at the age of twenty-five ?

Noi, who lives in the next village, has gone to work in a Chiang Mai massage parlour, to help support her son and her parents. She says it is a boring job that has become quite mechanical to her now; no worse, Noi says, than washing dirty clothes. She has friends among the other girls, lives better than ever she could at home, and sends her family money every month.

Lek went to work in a bar in Bangkok and thoroughly enjoys herself – the clothes she can afford, the music and the fun of the bar, the rich *farang* men, one of whom actually took her for a holiday in Singapore and wants to marry her, not knowing that she has three children – all this is a far cry from the life she would now be leading if she had stayed here.

I can not think that a girl who sells herself, either to help support her family, or to escape the grinding drudgery and boredom of village life, does wrong. But those who ensnare, imprison and live off others will, in their next lives, suffer as I have suffered; at times I have believed that in my previous life I must have been such a creature.

It is several days since last I wrote. Perhaps reaching back into a previous life, for so I consider the days before my fall, is something that should not be lightly undertaken. I must find out about those holy men who, I read in a magazine, clearly recall their earlier reincarnations.

The rains have ceased, the mountains have reappeared, covered in scrubby green with occasional bare, brown patches where the hilltribes, Meo I believe, have cleared the slopes to grow rice or, more likely, opium. In the distance towers Chiang Dow, its sheer sides and irregular top, for once not cloaked in clouds, looking like an ancient crown. The sky is washed a pale blue and in the evening changes to a wonderous clean yellow, then orange as the sun sets. There will be no more rain now until the mango showers in four months' time.

The cold winds are blowing softly from the north and I need a sweater in the morning and two blankets on my bed at night, although it is lovely to sit outside in the hot daytime sun. November, December and January are the best months of the year in Chiang Mai.

Let me try and draw a picture of our family compound. I have said that we live on the bank of the River Ping. A narrow, rutted cart track runs along the bank and then there is a thick tea hedge (not the tea you can drink or make *miang* from, but a bush with small green leaves) behind which lies our compound. In the front, standing high on four thick teak legs, is the rice store, the most important place in our compound and in our lives, as it is in the lives of all farmers. If at the end of the harvest the store is full then we know that, whatever other failures and troubles there may be, we can live securely for another year. If, on the other hand, it is not full enough then, towards, the end of the year, Chand and Tip will have to go away and try to find work. If they are lucky enough to get a job on a building site or road project, it will reduce by two the mouths to be fed and the money they send home will enable us to survive until the next harvest is gathered in. But sometimes families are forced to eat their seed corn and borrow money. If that happens, it is almost impossible for them ever to recover and the family will end up by selling its land to pay back the money-lenders who often charge interest of ten per cent a month. Sometimes, too, the children have to be given away or even sold. I talked once with my grandmother about this horrible practice. She told me that I must remember that in the past children had always been sold into slavery to pay their parents' debts and that, even now, girls were, in fact, always sold to their future husband's family who paid the girl's parents the cost of 'mother's milk' before they agreed to the marriage. Was this, she asked, so very different from selling them to a stranger? She said, no. I said, yes.

Behind the rice store is our house. It, like all the houses in the north, stands on thick teak posts. Teak is the best, of all woods, hard and long lasting it is not attacked by termites and, until recently, all houses were built with teak. Now it is difficult to find and very expensive. A steep ladder leads up to the porch where, on a shelf are two earthen jars full of rain water for drinking. Since the jars are slightly porous the water is cool even in the hottest weather. A half coconut with a long, carved wooden handle makes an excellent dipper and cup. It is a lovely and old custom in the north to put such jars outside your garden, beside the road, so that any wayfarer can refresh himself.

Inside the house it is rather dark as the window shutters are almost always closed in the heat of the day. The floor is made from long, wide planks of highly polished teak that grandfather cut himself in the forest across the river. On the left is a raised space where Chand now sleeps. High up,

13

above head height, is a shelf which is the Spirit Place. Although the place is for the Spirit of the family we also keep there a picture of Luang Por, two small vases and a statue of the Lord Buddha. In the bedroom, where we all slept as children with mother and father, there are two cupboards with looking-glass fronts where we keep all our clothes and personal possessions. Now only Tip sleeps with mother and father on their mats on the floor under the mosquito nets.

The living area is decorated with bright posters and coloured photographs of film stars from magazines (Chand has even put up a topless European girl) and of course there is a picture of the Royal Family. A glass cupboard contains a few family treasures. Bright stones Tip and I brought back from a day at Mae Sar waterfall, some needle work we did at school, cups and saucers and a few glasses. On top of the cupboard are the family photographs, father at a *wat* meeting, Chand in the army, Noi, my eldest sister, on her wedding day and myself in school uniform.

At the back of the house, black with smoke, is the kitchen. Two clay stoves heated with charcoal stand on a sand covered shelf, and above them are hung up various baskets and cooking utensils; on the right is a screened cupboard containing left-over food; its feet stand in dishes of water to keep out the ants.

Beside the kitchen is an open verandah with a shoulder-high wooden screen around it. This is the bathroom. In it are two large brown jars decorated with golden dragons which hold the well water we use for cooking and washing.

From the outside our house looks old and sturdy, the wooden walls dark with age and the clay roof tiles black with dirt. Now it has changed, but I always liked the open area under the house best of all. Here was a low platform covered with a woven mat on which we sat to talk or to work

14

while the chicken and dogs scratched in the dust. Farm equipment lay round-about – a wooden plough, a great winnowing basket, assorted tools and the buffalo cart with a fat, happy elephant carved on the back. Here we lay in the heat of the day and chatted with our friends in the cool of the evening.

Behind the house is our well with a bucket on the end of a long bamboo pole for drawing up the water. Our well has sweet water and, being so near the river, is never dry. Beside it is Tip's herb garden where she grows most of the ingredients for making curry pastes and other spicy dishes; three different kinds of chillies, majoram, basil, *takrai, bai toey* and so on. We also have a lime bush, two *lamyai* trees and *okrong* mango, so called because the fruit has a groove like the cleavage between a girl's breasts.

Noi, her husband Geow, and two children, a boy, Nit, aged three and a baby girl called Dam, live in a small bamboo house at the bottom of the compound. In the far corner is the lavatory that we all use. I have grown a few flowers; a sweet scented jasmine by the steps, bright red hibiscus and a riot of marigolds near the front entrance through the tea hedge. It is a friendly compound and I have come to love it very much. I no longer wish to be anywhere else.

I jumped, but I missed the lorry. Faces peered down at me as I lay, hundreds of faces and there was no sound and there was no colour in the world. I spun away into a black void.

The weeks in the Police Hospital passed in a daze of disbelief, disbelief that never again would I walk or control the lower part of my body which would forever hang broken and useless. My name was in the newspapers, a photograph of me lying on the road like a thrown-away doll. The owner of the brothel was arrested together with the mamasan. All the other girls were sent home, but Sak was never caught. I was told that the brothel gave the police Bts. 30,000 for me but I am sad to say that they kept more than half of it for their own – "expenses", the rest helped a little towards the cost of my stay in the hospital.

Many people came to visit me but I was too shocked to talk and they gave me no comfort, no hope. My parents made the long journey, having sold the buffalo, the bicycle and most of their rice to raise the money that would be needed for my expenses and the cost of their stay in Bangkok. They were lost and frightened in the big city and could do nothing to cheer me up. At last they pushed me in my wheelchair, a gift from someone who had come to see me– to this day I do not know who that kind person was – out of the hospital gate, all their money gone and a crippled girl to care for.

During the long journey home I stared out of the train window thinking of that carefree Bua Geow who had made the trip with such high hope so few weeks before. A free bird, caged, despoiled and broken. I could not see the future.

My brother carried me up the steep steps into our house and placed me on a mat on the raised space where he had always slept. It was November, the day of the Loy Kratong Festival when we had always dressed up in our best clothes, flowers in our hair and lipstick, rouge and eye-shadow all over our faces. We joined our friends at the *wat* which lay on the river bank at the other end of the village. We carried our *kratong*, made out of banana leaves and containing a candle, three incense sticks and a coin and together we pushed them out into the current where they mingled and jostled with all those others that floated down from the villages above, their candles burning, little star-beacons in the night. We wished as we launched them and thanked the spirit of the River for her bountiful waters and hoped that our sins or bad luck would pass from us with the departing *kratong*. On this one night, amidst the laughter of our friends, we believed.

Chand offered to push me to the *wat* in my wheelchair but I had no heart to join my friends in their happiness nor could I now believe. For months I moped upstairs; not only was I a useless burden but I had been the cause of my family crossing the narrow divide from one that was just self-sufficient to one that was in debt. We could not see how the debt could be paid back.

Often as I lay I thought of the spirit of the River and of making the short one way journey to join her. Only the love and sympathy of my family which they could not express but which, nevertheless, I felt, sustained me through those first weeks and the months that followed.

I did not read, for we had no books, I did not work, for what could I do ? I hardly ever went outside because this meant that Chand had to carry me downstairs and wait to carry me up again and he was always busy trying to earn extra money. After the first few days only one or two friends ever came to see me for I was not a cheerful person.

17

Buddhism, I have come to realise, offers little comfort to such as I. I must, I believed, have done evil in a previous life and to pay for that I had to suffer now. There is nothing anyone can do to change this fact, only can I pray that my present suffering will finally be considered to have offset my previous sin, if not in this life then, perhaps, in the next.

One day after I had been home for a year, a little old *farang* lady, dressed in white and grey was driven along the bumpy track to our house. She climbed the steep steps and immediately knelt down beside me and started praying in Thai saying that her God and his son Jesus cared more for one suffering person such as I than for a thousand people who could live a normal life. Later she told me that my accident was not a punishment but a misjudged jump. She told me that there were thousands of people paralysed like myself who lived active and useful lives. She came to see me several times and always made me feel much better. Once she brought five disabled girls from Chiang Mai in a pick-up truck to visit me, it was wonderful to talk to others who understood. Once or twice she became more serious and seemed to want me to accept her God instead of Buddha but I could not believe that the King and all Thai people, my parents and sisters, were wrong and would go to Hell while I would go to a Heaven full of *farang* and angels. I relapsed into my old state of hopelessness.

And then I noticed, but of course could not feel, sores on my bottom. Over the weeks they became worse, festering, smelly and I could see the bone, white and obscene. I could no longer sit up and I lay all day and all night on my stomach. There was no money to take me to a doctor and no one in the village could help. It was fate and the end, my end, would come soon as had been ordained. My family, although they never showed it, had decided I was dying. I gave up. I scarcely ate, and I prayed every time

I went to sleep that I should not wake again.

I have mentioned my family and described the compound where we live and now perhaps I should say a little about us all. My father's family lived in a village some miles up the river. His parents were poor farmers and after their death, when I was two years old, we only had occasional contact with his family. As is the custom, father came to live in mother's compound when they were married. Marriage in the north is very simple and does not involve either religious or civil ceremonies. Once the wedding had been approved by both sides, father paid a small sum of money to mother's family, or rather to the family spirits, built himself a bamboo house in the compound, and moved in. My mother took his surname, but this is hardly ever used– only for official purposes. When my grandfather was born no one in Thailand had a surname and I read the other day that it was King Rama VI who, in 1913, ordered everyone to have a surname as they did in the West. I noticed when I was in Chiang Mai that telephone directories list people under their first name and not under their surname. Even this can be confusing as people sometimes change their name to a more lucky one and, of course, everyone has a nickname which is always used by their friends.

Father brought no rice fields with him, so he came very much under the authority of mother's parents who lived in the main house that I have already described. Grandfather died when I was young and I scarcely remember him but my grandmother I loved dearly and it was her quiet wisdom and acceptance of the rhythm and hardship of life that has helped me, so I believe, to endure the past years. Bent and small, I remember her always with flowers. Her delight was to potter round the compound watering and tending the herbs and flowers. Every week on *wan pra* or

19

Holy Day she would make a delicate arrangement of flowers and hobble off to the *wat* carrying them on a tray. She would spend the day gossiping with her friends and return in the evening happily full of stories and scandal from the village.

As we sat under the house in the evening grandmother would tell us stories, stories from the history and fables of Queen Chamadevi, Haripunchai and of the Kingdom of Lan Na which, in the old days, stretched far and wide from its capital at Chiang Mai. She told us of the spirits of the rivers and mountains but she never let us be frightened and she did not believe in ghosts that were deliberately malicious. Most of all she talked of life and how to cope with it, how to make oneself and other people happy. It is only very recently that I have come to realise that she was, in fact, explaining the very essence of the Buddhist religion, although, if she had been told so, she would have denied it, since she had had no education and could not read or write.

When she died, quietly in her sleep, I was thirteen years old. I mourned her deeply and with her went, I feel, one of the last of those who embodied the unchanging, unhurried tradition that was the fabric of old Lan Na. Modern communications, television, wirelesses, motorbikes, Bangkok and Western influences, all these have destroyed grandmother's way of life and beliefs.

Buffalo and ox-carts were, until yesterday, it seems, a central part of our lives. As a child I often looked after our buffalo, leading him out to graze in the early mist of morning, lying half-asleep on his back in the heat of the day and taking him for his afternoon wallow in the muddy creek. I would walk beside father as he ploughed our water-logged field shouting "*kwa! kwa!*" for all buffaloes veer to the left for some reason known only to themselves. At

20

harvest time we would come back from the rice fields, as the sun set, along the deep rutted track, tired but happy, the cart laden with golden grain, its great wheels creeking *"id, od, ad; id, od, ad"* as they lurched over the bumps.

Those days are gone forever. Now carts are as rare as honest policemen. The wheels have been sold as decoration for restaurants and vulgar pick-up trucks roar down the lanes trailing clouds of coughing dust and forcing people into the ditch.

Now, too, teak is impossible to get and wood of any kind is very expensive so that more and more houses are built of bricks and cement squatting like ugly cake boxes on the ground. *Sa-Ou* (Saudi Arabia) houses we call them since many are built and owned by workers who have returned from there or who send money home. Uncomfortable, hot and foreign looking, I do not like them at all.

But the greatest change that ever came to our village was brought about by the arrival of electricity a few years ago. We used to rise when the sun did and sleep when it went away for the night – not any more.

Of course I know all about electricity. There is lots of it in the big towns. In Bangkok we lay and stared at the naked bulbs hanging starkly above us, lighting up the cobwebs in the corners and the *chingchok* waiting for their supper – the squalor of that brothel room.

In Mae Khun's house there were lights everywhere, cheerful in the evening and keeping burglars and ghosts away at night. Electric machines worked silently in every room fans, televisions, refrigerators, mixers, blenders, toasters and even a rice-cooker in the kitchen. They were taken for granted. They were just there.

But here in our village ? I didn't think it would be right, that it would, as it were, grow well here anymore than grapes would. Yet it has come and we treat it as something quite natural. I remember it all started with much coming and going of officials who held meetings with the village elders, went around sticking pegs in the ground and daubing red marks on the trees. It came by wire, high-up on concrete posts and will kill you if it catches you. No one seems to know where it comes from, why it is willing to enter our house when I press a switch or where it goes to when I turn it off. I suppose they must have found some left-over stock in Chiang Mai. The schoolteacher says that there are two kinds of electricity – the water kind and the black kind that comes from a great hole near Lampang. It is like wet rice and hill rice I think.

They came one day in lorries and cut down all the lovely old rain trees (we used to sit under their cool, green shade and in March, I remember, when the new leaves came out, drops of moisture fell on us as if it was really raining). Those aged trees that towered to the left and to the right of the road that winds up to the school are gone now, alas!

I cried when they killed the one near our house. With screeching saws they first cut off its limbs one by one. Finally they felled the trunk at ground level below the blood red mark they had made. No one but me seemed to mind since the villagers were allowed to take away all the small branches to use as fuel. The big pieces were loaded by crane onto a lorry under the supervision of Pu Yai and See who had presumably made special arrangements with the electricity men. I suppose they will sell all the wood to the carvers in Chiang Mai and make a lot of money for themselves although the trees rightfully belonged to all of us.

Concrete posts were stuck in the ground beside the road where the pegs had been placed. There is one near our front gate which spoils the view of the mountain. Great cotton reels of wire were unwound, strung along from post to post and pulled tight. Certainly its coming has not added to the beauty of the village but it must be a good thing even though we have managed perfectly well without it in the past. I wonder how much it will cost ?

Well now I know! The *Pu Yai's* son came round and told us that he was the sole agent for the meters (a gadget that counts the electricity as it comes into our house) and we must buy one before electricity is allowed to enter. He is also, apparently, the only person who can pull the wire from the meter and install the neon lights and plugs that we will need. He looked around and told father that we could have two plugs and three lights. The total cost will be Bahts 2,500 equal to 330 kilos of garlic!

He kindly said that we only had to pay half now, the rest we could pay in instalments, and on this balance he would only charge ten per cent interest a month. Of course father had to agree and he also promised to give him the title-deeds of our land as security.

The village is all lit up! It looks very different and will, I am sure, change all our lives. For one thing I will be able to do my cross-stitch work in the evening which I really couldn't do with the dim shaky light of an oil-lamp. With everyone watching television I expect, too, that there will be fewer babies.

See has declared open house so that everyone can inspect all the electrical equipment that he has. Black and white and coloured television sets, radios, electric fans, refrigerators, irons and rice-cookers. For three days we can go and admire his wealth, free of charge, after that we will have to pay to watch the television.

I might have guessed that there was more to See's generosity than met the eye. He is the agent for all the pieces of equipment we saw in his house and he is now going around the village selling them and most people will buy because their neighbours do and what is the point of having electricity if they don't ? Father has bought a black and white television set and a fan. He will pay for them over the next two years plus, of course, ten per cent interest a month. It turns out that the use of the electricity costs us about a hundred baht each month. Electricity may be a good thing but it has certainly milked the poorer villagers of any surplus cash they might earn. But never mind See and *Pu Yai* are surely much richer.

And there is another thing. Most of us will have seen television at one time or another in the town, but it is quite a different matter to have a set permanently on in your own home. Suddenly the elders are talking knowledgeably about Bosnia and the American Presidential election whereas before anything outside the village was beyoud their reach.

The young people are ensnared by the high fashion and highlife of the Bangkok soap operas with their flashy cars and glittering women; the advertisements promising instant success and wealth if you use their product. This worries me very much as it makes our life in the village seem so dull and drab. I sense that many of the young people, especially the girls, are restless and dissatisfied with their life here in a way that they never were before. They want to live like the people they see and own the things that they own; they know that they can't if they stay here. But they have so little education that they will only get work in Bangkok or Chiang Mai on building sites. Unless, they do of their own free will what I was forced to do. I fear, too, that not all parents will object. Farming has become more mechanical, labour, particularly the labour of girls, is less in demand. On top of this many families are now deeply in debt having borrowed more than they can ever hope to repay. The silken tongues of people like Sak, offering a large lump sum in cash and a steady income from their daughter in the future are, in a crisis, hard for parents to resist. Although I am certain none in our village would ever agree. Electricity and other modern inventions have not brought only blessings to the villagers.

Whilst I am in the mood for preaching let me also mention the question of land. Now there are four kinds of land – wet paddy fields where we grow rice in the rainy season and garlic in the cool season, dry land where it is possible to grow something such as soya beans, the village land where we live and the common forest where we hunt and gather wild plants.

Land as such has never had any money value. It is inherited, rented and sometimes lost to pay a debt but until very recently it would never have occured to anyone that it was worth money except for the crop that grew on it. But two years ago there were strange goings on in the next village down the river. Foreigners from Bangkok came and, working with the *Pu Yai* and the schoolmaster, they began to buy up land offering what seemed incredibly high prices. Few could resist the temptation, even though *puyai ban* and the schoolmaster took up to 40% for their commission. Those who sold a year later made even more.

Now great work is going on and there will be a resort golf course, whatever that may be. Everyone is happy. Perhaps a million baht in the bank, a life of lazy luxury, a pick-up truck, a television and no more hard work.

But we villagers can not save money, so that in a short while it will have gone and then what will they and what will their children do ?

Por Khun says it is inevitable thay many, many people will have to leave the land and go to work in the towns. It happened in his country years ago and many of the country people did very well. He says what we need is education and training so that we can find good jobs and so that the girls will not be forced to do what I was forced to do.

Mother's brothers and sisters, ten in all, are widely scattered and although we see them and our cousins from time to time, helping those who still live in the village at harvest time and meeting them at important festivals, my family is not close to them at all, and when I remember Sak I am not sorry for this.

Mother inherited seven *rai* of good rice fields behind the village and this was enough for our small family when extra income from the second cash crop of garlic or beans was added. Father worked hard during the planting and harvesting of the two crops; and during the long, hot dry season when there was nothing to do on the land, he would try to find odd jobs in the village. Father is not very clever, and how should he be ? He did not go to school, nor did mother. He can not compete in village politics and seems to have learned nothing from the many government officials who have been here to advise on how to improve farming methods and crop yield. At home father talks little and Chand is more and more taking over responsibility for the family.

Chand is now twenty-five and I hope, selfishly, that he does not marry, for if he does, he will certainly have to move to his wife's compound and will no longer be able to help father very much. Before I went to Bangkok I worshipped Chand for he was always kind to me. Sometimes he took me with him when he visited his friends, but usually he put on his best clothes and went off with a group of boys to visit and chat-up the girls in the tradition word-play game of the northern villages. This is a game in which the boy and girl make outrageously sexual remarks to each other and express their hopes of love by using totally different words which sound nearly the same. The words are often concerned with food such as, "Did you have pumpkin curry for supper tonight ?" which means "Do you love me ?" Since the word for pumpkin is 'fak' and the word for love is 'rak'. Although this is a game, it is also very serious and is the way in which boys and girls find out about each other and their feelings, become regular friends and finally marry. As the village communities are small and so open, there is much pressure from the family spirits to stop boys and girls sleeping together before they are married although, of course, it can and does happen.

One of the reasons why Lynn wanted to come to Bangkok with me, I learned later, was because she had fallen in love with a boy and slept with him in their rice store. He had several other girl friends and never came to see Lynn again. To make matters worse, her mother found out that she had lost her virginity and forced her to apologise in front of everyone to the family spirits.

Some years ago Chand fell in love with the third daughter of our *puyai baan* or village headman but when he was formally approached by father, he refused to give his consent as our family was too poor. Chand was deeply hurt and has not had a serious girlfriend since.

My sister, Noi, married Geow who comes from a very poor family that lives in the forest across the River and survives by making and selling charcoal. Geow is not a very successful member of our family group. He helps father in the fields when he has to, otherwise he finds the occasional labouring job and then spends the money he has earned drinking Mekhong or rice wine. I feel very sorry for Noi, she has to work so hard and yet often she can scarcely feed her children let alone buy them any little luxuries like sweets or toys. She gets up at four o'clock every morning and catches the five o'clock mini-bus from the village to Chiang Mai. There she sits all day on the pavement near the

Gard Luang Market, selling *kanom* that she and Tip make in the evening. Sometimes what she earns does not even cover the bus fare.

The two children Nit and especially Dam, the baby, are a joy to me and I spend hours with them. It is terrible that I do not like to be left alone with them, but what could I do if anything were to happen ? And the River is so close.

Tip has been wonderful to me. She it is who helps me in the lavatory and with all the other personal matters that I can not do by myself. She sits with me whenever she is free from her work in the fields and I help her with the *kanom* and do some sewing for her. She washes my clothes, cleans my room and cheers me up more than anyone else. It is strange that only one of us has married and that my parents only have two grandchildren.

I had not seen my mother's eldest sister since before I went to Bangkok; she worked as a cook in Chiang Mai and never came to visit us. We had heard that she and her dog, Pook, had recently gone to live in a grand *farang* house, but that was all we knew. Mother had been ill and someone in the village told my aunt, and her new employers brought her to visit mother.

So it was that Mae Khun and Por Khun came up to see me as I lay on my stomach in the gloom, doing nothing and thinking of nothing. Mother by this time was quite well and had gone to the fields, only Tip was at home. They sat beside me, the *farang* and his Thai wife, I told them a little about myself in a listless way and finally showed them my bottom. I had been poked about in my helplessness so much in the hospital that I am no longer shy about my useless lower body, it is no more to me than a wooden leg would be.

There is a bird in our old stories that burns itself and then rises anew from its own ashes. On this day, September 7th in the nineteenth year of my life, just over three years since I went to Bangkok, I started my new life.

Mae Khun insisted that I should go with them immediately to see a doctor in Chiang Mai and, to my own surprise, for I had long since lost all will to do anything, I agreed. Tip collected a few things for me to take, saying that she would tell my parents when they came home and then follow to look after me. Once again I set off with my few possessions in a plastic bag, a very different feeling in my heart but nevertheless a feeling, or at least a stirring that had been absent for so very long.

Once more a hospital, doctors and surgery; after ten days I emerged with a new bottom that I was assured would be good for many a long year provided I treated it with respect and did not sit on it for too many hours at a time. I wheeled myself from the car into Mae Khun's house on a

29

fine sunny morning, the sky washed clean after a week of rain. All the colours looked fresher than I could remember ever having seen them. The new leaves on the mango trees, a soft brownish yellow, contrasting with the dark green of the old leaves. The *lamyai* trees, a more sober green and splashes of red and white bougainvillea. Beyond the garden, Phrathat Doi Suthep perched white and gold on top of the hazy mountain which undulates across the sky.

I felt like running. But I never could and my joy dropped from me like a wet *pasin*. Life would not change, I would go home to lie in my gloomy upstairs room with a ladder down which I would never climb.

"What are we going to do with you now ?" Mae Khun startled me by asking the very question I was pondering. We sat on the lawn and the evening colours were still bright, even though the sun had dipped to hide behind Doi Sutep, filling the sky with the red warning of its going.

It was decided that I should go and live in a sewing school for disabled girls in the grounds of the Roman Catholic Church. Twelve girls live there and do enough sewing to pay for their keep, although I believe the Sisters help out from time to time. It was some of these girls who had once come to visit me. Next day I went and although Pensri, who runs the school, herself unable to walk, was very kind to me, I was not happy. Mostly, I think, because I could not look after myself and had to rely on other girls less handicapped than myself. Only Tip can help me in these matters without embarrassment. Also at the back of my mind was the memory that it was in order to save up and buy a sewing machine that I went to Bangkok. After two days I sent a message to Mae Khun asking her to take me home, for I was homesick, too.

First she spent a day showing me how to do cross-stitch work. This I found I enjoyed and could do easily. So with a box of material and thread I returned to my home by the River, to the familiar sounds of barking dogs and scratching hens, to the smells of cooking and to my family.

Mae Khun talked to father and said that she would give him the money with which to build a room for me underneath the house. Within three weeks it was finished. The floor is smooth concrete, there is a bedroom, a bathroom and a dayroom. I can now wheel myself about from room to room and out into the compound. How wonderful it is! I have put up posters on the white-washed walls, curtains on the windows and photographs on a shelf. I have two cupboards, one in the bedroom for my clothes and one in the dayroom where I keep my cross-stitch material and a few other nick-nacks. There is also a table at which I work and a bench for guests.

I was free to move about, to go outside when I wanted to instead of having to be carried downstairs. It felt almost as if I were free from the prison of my immobility. I began to care which clothes I wore; I brushed and put ribbons in my hair; I looked in the looking-glass and saw a pale but pretty face with half a smile, a great improvement on the hopeless, sunken-eyed girl who had lost all interest in life only a few weeks ago.

One day Mae Khun arrived with four beautiful little cross-stitch figures of hilltribe girls in their gay traditional costumes Lisu, Meo, Yao and Akha. She told me that my work would be made into Christmas cards, that she would give me all the material and pay me four baht for each figure I made and that if there was any profit from selling the cards it would go to help other girls like myself.

This, to me, seemed a marvellous idea as I now had regular work that I enjoyed doing. I found I could easily sew

31

five a day and this made me feel that I was helping my family again instead of being a useless burden. It was also good to think that I was helping other unfortunate girls by my work.

I have now reached the point in this diary when I have caught up with myself, with the present, as it were. Here I am at home working and content, thanks to the strange intervention of two strangers. A new life has started. Whatever I did wrong in a previous life must, I believe, now have been paid for in full. Tomorrow I will write only of the present and the future.

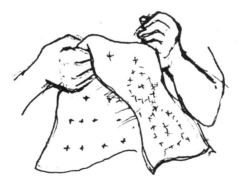

I have decided that this day, December 9th, the second full moon of the northern year, shall be my birthday. I am twenty years old today.

I have always felt that I was missing something because my parents could not remember on which day I was born – they associated my arrival with garlic and cold weather, that was all. At school I was often teased, but looking back, I suspect that many other children did not really know either, and had simply made up a date, as now I have done.

This morning I made myself a cross-stitch picture of a girl wearing a white dress with black hair down to the ground. In her hands was a box that she had just been given as a surprise birthday present. I stuck the picture into a card and wrote on it "Happy birthday to Bua Geow from all the world" and gave it to myself after lunch.

In the afternoon I went for a walk in my wheelchair along the lane towards the village. It was the first time I had ever ventured out alone and my heart raced with excitement, although the unaccustomed exercise may have had something to do with it too. Tari was sitting beneath her house sewing; when she saw me she ran out and pulled me laughing into the compound calling out for her family to come and meet their new visitor. When I told them that it was my birthday Tari rushed to the village shop and came back with a bag of *kanom* and several bottles of Coca-Cola it was the best of birthday parties. I showed Tari and her sister, Nongnai, the cross-stitch work I was doing and they asked if they could make some too. They have both just finished school and have very little to do at home during the slack months between seedtime and harvest. I promised to ask Mae Khun because I know that otherwise they will certainly leave home to look for work in Chiang Mai or Bangkok. They both have a good education and so should fare better than I did but there are many dangers and temptations and it would be good if they can stay at home.

A worried Chand came looking for me, stayed a while to flirt with Tari, until she stood up, swept back her hair, raised her left eyebrow, smiled and walked away. He then pushed a tired but happy me home as the moon rose up on the right and the sun sank glowering behind the mountains beyond the river.

When next Mae Khun came I had one hundred hilltribe figures to give to her Bts.400 for less than three weeks' work, if you can call doing something you enjoy work. This is as much as father often earns in a month doing odd jobs for people in the village. I spoke of Tari's interest and Mae Khun said she thought it would be possible to sell more cards over the next few weeks because of Christmas and New Year. She asked me to teach them and make certain that they did it correctly. She hoped to be able to sell enough cards overseas to keep all of us working most, if not all, of the time. She says she will not pay Tari and her sister as much as she does me since they should be able to make twice as many in a day as I can; that sounds fair to me.

I had been thinking about poor Pun whom I have not seen since before I went to Bangkok as she lives in a village on the other side of the valley. Eight years ago when she was nineteen, she went to work in a textile factory near Bangkok. I met her a few times when she came home for the Songkran or Loy Kratong holidays; she seemed very content and was able to send money to her mother every month. Her younger sister went to work in the same place and soon afterwards we heard that she was going to marry a soldier.

They drove back late at night after the wedding party. Pun and her sister, the bride, sat in front of a pick-up truck driven by a friend of the groom who had been drinking

Mekhong steadily all evening. He can never have seen the ten-wheel truck parked, without lights, at the side of the road and slammed into its back. He and Pun's sister were killed instantly. Pun was trapped, crushed and partly conscious in the wreck for three hours before they cut her free. Miraculously she lived but she was blinded in one eye and both her legs had to be amputated above the knee. She came home and lived with her mother until four years ago when we heard, with much amazement, that she had married Geow, a lazy, good-for-nothing from a nearby village, and had moved into a tumbled-down house owned by his family. He turned out to be worse than we had feared. Drunk whenever he managed to earn some money, he would often beat Pun for not feeding him properly, yet he gave her scarcely enough money to buy even rice, and what could the poor girl do to help ? It is only through the charity of her family that she survives. I am told that she no longer bothers to look after herself, is dirty, bad-tempered and has lost all her old friends.

It seemed to me that she had given up, just as once I had done. I told her story to Mae Khun and Por Khun and they said they would go to see her on their next visit.

I awoke this morning feeling excited, although at first I could not think why, then I remembered that I was going to teach Tari and Nongnai how to do cross-stitch work. I felt very important as I got ready the thread, needles and cloth – me a teacher! We spent a happy day together and, as I suspected, they were both very quick to learn and will certainly be able to make many more pieces than I can, but then I can not sit for too long and I need to rest as I quickly feel tired. I asked Tari to go and see Pun and find out if she is interested or able to do this work too.

Por Khun's house in Chiang Mai is full of old pots and dishes. He told me a little about them and showed me a book he had written with photographs of many of the pieces I could see in the cupboards, but it was in English so I could not read it. He has ceramics from many countries, from China, Vietnam and Cambodia, but most come from the old Thai kingdoms of Sukothai and Lan Na and were made, he says, five or six hundred years ago. Many of the pieces were found in graves in Indonesia; apparently Thai or Chinese merchants, all those years ago, exported tens of thousands of pieces and several junks have been found on the seabed with the cargo of ceramics still intact. The natives of Indonesia had the custom of burying their dead and placing pots, vases and dishes in the grave filled with food and drink for the long journey to heaven and, perhaps, as gifts with which to bribe the authorities on their arrival. His house must be full of ghosts although, I must admit, I did not feel anything bad when I stayed there.

Por Khun says that there were many kilns in old Lan Na here in the north of Thailand. Some of the pieces he showed me are very lovely; my favourites are the soft cloud-grey coloured ones with black decoration from Kalong which is half way between Chiang Mai and Chiengrai.

There are also some lovely chestnut brown vases from Phayao. He says there must be many grave sites in Lan Na, full of buried treasure, waiting to be found. I was telling all this to Chand last week when suddenly he interrupted me.

"I found some bits of broken pottery, some bronze bowls and bones in our riverside field last year. I wonder if it is a grave full of gold," he said jokingly.

"Why not go and find out. The exercise will do you good," I replied.

He came home next evening with two ceramic bowls with birds painted black in the middle which looked very much like the Kalong pieces I had seen in Por Khun's house and a lime pot with lime still inside it. Tari happened to be with me and said she would like to go and watch Chand dig. I knew that Por Khun was coming next day so Tari and I decided to ask him to take us as it is possible to get there by car.

So it was that Por Khun lifted me out of the car and so it was that I placed his hand on my heart. I would like to set down what he wrote about that day in his notes.

"It is not easy for me to write of my feelings for Bua Geow, but I must, in all honesty, say that sympathy for a pretty innocent child, despoiled and crippled, a child whom we had been able to help and make happy again, that this sympathy was tinged with some deeper, more primitive feeling not normally associated with a crusty, happily married university lecturer. Bua Geow's feelings I did not know.

"I carried her from the car and found to my embarrassment that my left hand was pressed just below, and was in contact with, her breast; I had only walked a few steps when I felt a little warm hand creeping down my arm, it fastened onto my index finger, lifted my hand upwards and placed it firmly over her breast. In consternation I stumbled and my hand involuntarily grasped that upon which it lay. By good luck Tari arrived at that very moment with the wheelchair and I was able to release my burden. Bua Geow smiled and squeezed my hand as I placed her gently in her chair. My feeling were not those of a scholar, and I have resolved to be more circumspect in my future handling of that young lady."

It was not until several weeks later that Mae Khun read his notes to me. When she reached this passage she paused, looked straight at me and smiled before she began to translate what he had written.

Blood rushed to my face and, if I had been able, I would have run from the room to hide in shame. I hastened to

37

explain that he had quite misunderstood, that it was purely an accident that his hand had ended up where it did; she hushed me, said it was quite all right, she understood and was glad. She went on translating as if nothing had happened.

But it had not been an accident. That night I lay long awake thinking about the two of them and what they meant to me. Por Khun is fifty and going grey, where he is not already bald. He likes to give the impression that he is a stiff and serious scholar. At first we were afraid of him and laughed at him behind his back. But then I came to realise that this was all an act. Once you are able to laugh at him openly and laugh with him, his cover falls away and he become a warm, childlike person and instead of being a distant father figure, he became innocent and vulnerable, someone even I could, I felt, help and protect. I have never known love outside my own family, only rape, but my feelings for Por Khun are certainly something I have never known before and can not describe. Yes, I think I badly wanted to be touched by him. No, it had not been an accident.

And Mae Khun, how shall I describe her ? Those she does not like should beware, to those she helps she gives wisdom, sympathy and understanding. She, it was who gave me back my self-respect. She pushed father and Chand into planting a second crop and lent them money with which to do it. She made them build my room so that they believed it was their idea and their work, but in fact it was her idea and her money.

Some weeks later I received a beautifully typed letter from someone in Lampun who said that he was paralysed from the waist down as the result of a car crash. He lived with his mother, who came from Bangkok, and had taught himself to type; he asked if we could be pen friends. His name was Pan and so a new interest entered my life. One day Mae Khun casually asked how Pan was; now I had never mentioned his name to her so I knew that it was she who had first prompted him to write to me. She had understood my need for outside contact, why I had reached out for Por Khun and how vulnerable he was, and she had determined to find another, safer friend with whom I could share, and to whom I could unburden, my innermost thoughts and feelings.

When finally we reached the site we saw Chand and three friends digging near the bank of the river. We sat and watched, Por Khun the while giving unnecessary advice.I won't write about the dig as it wasn't very exciting. Anyway Por Khun has already talked about it endlessly to anyone who would listen. I am sticking in my diary something he wrote although I can't read it nor could I understand it when he translated it for me.

When finally we reached the site we saw Chand and three friends digging near the bank of the river. We sat and watched, Por Khun the while giving unnecessary advice.

I noticed that Tari was becoming increasingly restless. Suddenly she jumped to her feet. She stood above them where they dug, motionless and eerily beautiful, one arm outstretched towards Chand.

"I command you to stop immediately. You must not defile the resting place of She who is of the lineage of Chamadevi. Give that Seal to me and come up."

In awe Chand handed something to her that he had just found and silently, like chastened children, they climbed out of the hole. Por Khun and I stared in wonder at this girl whom we did not know. She stood awhile holding whatever it was clasped tightly in her fist and then walked away as if in a dream.

Later she came sheepishly to my house and gave what had been found to Por Khun. He went outside and washed it. When he came back he was frowning with concentration and from his fingers, on a slender gold chain hung a cloud-grey coloured ceramic elephant.

"It it a seal from the kalong kilns," he said. "The writing is in ancient script but I think it says 'the Seal of Tammatari.' How did you know it was a seal?" he asked Tari.

"Because it is mine, Sydney," she replied taking it back. She turned and left without another word.

"Sydney!" he said. "Sydney? Why did she call me that?"

We felt uncomfortable and puzzled.

The garlic is growing nicely and we hear that the price should be good. Also we have more than enough rice to last us through the year. At the start of the season father borrowed Bht. 10,000 interest free from Mae Khun and with that sum he has been able to plant and fertilize seven *rai* of garlic as well as paying off all his old debts on which he was paying 10% interest a month. Now even the Bts. 10,000 has been cleared in full for Por Khun cancelled the debt in return for the ceramic and bronze pieces Chand found in the grave. That means that all we earn from this year's garlic crop will be sheer profit. We are already planning how to spend it: a television set for me, a motorbike for Tip, new clothes for mother and father and, we jokingly say, a bride for Chand. We will also build a barn behind the house where we can store next year's garlic crop and wait before we sell it until the price goes up. And toys for Nit and Dam.

Mother now goes regularly to the *wat* and from her gossip when she comes home (so like my grandmother) I gather that she has been accepted into the inner circle of friends of the *puyai baan's* wife. What a change in the position of our family from the days when the *puyai baan* rejected Chand's friendship with his daughter! I sometimes wonder if our fortune can hold or whether the spirits only allow a certain ration of happiness before bringing us down again to the harsh truth of life.

The King and Queen are coming to our village next month! The Abbot of our *wat* is greatly venerated in the area because he is able to tell the future. By this I do not mean that he predicts lottery numbers or reads people's palms, but that he will, at certain times and with certain people suddenly and for no reason, utter a prophesy that always turn out to be true. Many years ago my grandmother took me to see him when I was just a baby.

41

"Don't let her jump," was all he said

He often says much more important things than that and generals come to visit him. Then we know they are planning a coup. Luang Por, as we call him, will soon be eighty four years old and, although he is very frail, his mind is still clear and sharp. Their Majesties will come on his birthday. Imagine the excitement in the village! The *puyai baan* has set up a committee to make all the arrangements and father is on it which makes him feel very important. Mother and Tip will help with the floral decorations.

It is not easy for me to express what the King means to all of us who live in the countryside. We belong to Him, we know that He loves us and cares for us as a father should (but so often does not) but much more so, for this is His country, the land and all that dwell in it are His to dispose of as He sees fit, for He is the Lord of Life. Although the laws have changed since the end of Absolute Monarchy in 1932, our worship of the King has not. We know well that He is but a very human man, sometimes ill, sometimes disappointed, but in many ways He is to us as a God. All officials, police and government employees, seem only to come between us and the King, we see so little that they do to help, so much to trouble. Only when He comes to see us do we know that good will follow. Already it can be felt like wind before a storm; the road, rutted and pot-holed for years, has been repaired, the delapidated roof of the *wat* replaced and the walls newly painted. A constant stream of officials, who normally never bother to visit us, now come to see that all the preparations are proceeding smoothly. People in the village who have not spoken to each other for years are working cheerfully together. I have been told that I can sit in the *wat* compound very near to where the King will meet the *puyai baan*.

Dear Pan,

It was the fourth time in as many weeks that the poor postman has had to make the long journey to our house, but he is surely the only one who will complain; if you write every day I shall be seven times as happy as I am now, if that is possible, when I receive your weekly letter.

How wonderful that one of your stories has been published in the newspaper, perhaps you should write another one about our cross-stitch greeting cards so that more people will buy them and then more girls can earn money from making them!

Our house has been in turmoil for the past few weeks and it is now only two days until the King's visit. Father, well-dressed and erect, goes off to meetings all day instead of sleeping; they waste so much time talking I wonder how anything gets done, but they assure me all will be ready on the day. Mother spends hours practicing her flower decorating and tomorrow she, Tip and the other ladies will be up all night making the real decorations at the *wat*. No one has time to look after Nit and Dam and they pass most of their days with me, Nit is now quite clever at sewing although Dam is still too young and simply ties the threads up into untieable knots. I have to shoo them away in the afternoons when it is time for me to rest and this worries me as the River is so close, but there is nothing I could do to help if they fall in. I find I can only sit up and work for two or three hours at a time, then I begin to feel weak and tired and need to lie down and sleep for a while. I expect your are much stronger, or do you rest too?

I told you that I had been keeping a diary so you see I also am a kind of writer. But writing to you is so much better, I feel that I touch you through my words, and I don't even know what you look like! Please will you send me your photograph ?

My brother Chand is behaving strangely these days. He dresses very smartly, combs and oils his hair a lot and disappears at odd times for no good reason. He says that he is busy making arrangements for The Day, but I happen to know that this is not true. He must have a girlfriend and I will have to find out who she is.

Here I am chattering on about our family affairs as if I had known you all my life, and I must confess that the arrival of a letter from you does more to cheer me up than would a visit from all my aunts and uncles put together.

Enclosed, together with all my best wishes, is a jasmine flower from the bush outside my door, I planted it myself last year.

Your friend for ever,
Bua Geow

I am going to keep copies of all my letters to Pan, they give me much pleasure to write and are rather like a diary as I tell him about our family affairs and what I am doing. It is strange how much more alive I feel these days, as if drops of colour had fallen into the water of my world.

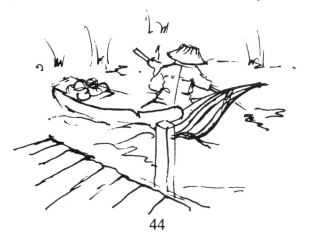

Is it because of this people have started coming to me for advice, or is it the other way round ? Nongnai and Tari came this morning bringing with them the work that they have done. I am making blue figures, they the red and green. Nongnai is so very small, but alert and alive with big round eyes over an upturned smile of a mouth; she wants to go to the Teachers' Training College in Chiang Mai and has been accepted because her school results were so good, but she now learns that there are too many teachers and she would not get a job when she graduated. I doubt, too, if her parents could afford her fees and expenses.

Tari is so different, tall and beautiful, as she very well knows, her long, black hair waterfalls down to her waist and sets off the clear whiteness of her skin. She has a typical northern Thai face, a large forehead, thick eyebrows and what Chand, who has seen too many Western films, calls a kissable mouth. She seems content to do as little as possible until the right man comes along to look after her but I wonder if I really know her. Today she was even more vague than usual, often forgetting to sew and staring into space. Is it a coincidence that I have noticed two people behaving in an odd way ?

Tari tells me that Mae Khun went to see Pun and was delighted when she knew that she had already started practicing cross-stitch work. It took her some time to get it right and this is scarely surprising since she has only one eye – I tried sewing with one eye shut and could not get the needle to go in the right place at all. Now she is making ten a day, twice as many as lazy I can do. At that rate she will be able to support her useless husband.

What a great day it has been for me and for the village! We were all up before daybreak, except for mother and her friends who never went to bed. I spent an hour washing and brushing my hair, then Tip came to help me dress and we argued again over what I should wear although we had discussed it for days and the chosen *pasin* and blouse were already ironed and laid out. The main problem was ribbons. These were very important as I knew that I would be sitting conspicuously in the front and might be seen by Their Majesties.

Finally we were ready and made our way down the lane into the village. Everything was so neat and tidy. The road had been swept and every house had a red, white and blue flag fluttering in the cool morning breeze; many had arches skillfully woven from banana leaves or royal greetings made out of straw. I hardly recognised the inside of the *wat*. The cloisters had been tidied up. The pile of roof tiles, the broken chairs and old water bottles had been removed, there was a new cupboard full of pieces from the grave that Por Khun had given to the Abbot and the newly white-washed walls dazzled where the sun reached them. Most of the courtyard is covered with sand that people give to make merit, but flowers – asters and petunias – had been planted beside the entrance to the *viharn* which stands glittering in the middle of the courtyard. It is not an old building but it has been well built. The roof is covered with glazed tiles, orange and green; the columns, doors and windows are decorated with coloured glass, made into floral and animal designs. Mother's flower arrangements had been hung around the cloisters and over the entrance arch; they looked very lovely.

By eleven o'clock everyone was in their place. The village elders and important visitors under their awning, the rest sitting on mats all around the courtyard. I had been put just beside the important people, right in the front. It was a good feeling, all of us quietly together waiting for a great event. I felt proud of our village, even the children were quiet, there was a sense of togetherness. This is our village, our *wat* and we are waiting, confident that we have done our best, to pay our respect to our Lord.

She spoke to me! The Queen spoke to me! They came, not as I had so often imagined with heralds bearing standards, with soldiers in magnificent uniforms, preceeded by trumpets and drums. We had been waiting since mid-morning chatting quietly amongst ourselves, for all was ready, when: there they were, two ordinary people walking quickly through the archway into the *wat* compound; no fuss, no ceremony, no warning; we were speechless and everyone prostrated themselves, except for poor me who was left sitting in solitary embarrassment. She, the Queen, was oh! so radiantly beautiful, a vision in pink, half hidden under a great white hat. He, the King, so simply dressed, in dark trousers and an open neck white shirt; he was bare-headed, wore dark glasses and carried a map in his hand.

They talked for some minutes to the *puyai baan* and I saw the King look at his map and make some notes. I guessed that they were discussing the new reservoir. The group of uncomfortable village elders in their new clothes sat behind the *puyai baan* on rented red chairs under a blue awning. Father kept rubbing his nose. Their Majesties moved towards the *viharn* where Luang Por, the Abbot, was awaiting them.

The Queen stopped right in front of me and asked what I was doing. To pass the time I had brought my work with me and in my surprise at the unexpected arrival of Their Majesties, I had forgotten to put it away and it was still lying on my lap. I heard a small and distant voice say: "Your Majesty, I am making cross-stitch hilltribe designs that will

47

be put into greeting cards." The Queen turned to one of her ladies-in-waiting and said: "Thongtip, I think these are lovely, please make a note for me as I would like to order some for myself and perhaps we can sell them in the Chitralada shops."

She then asked me if there was anything I needed and I managed to reply, "Your Majesty, I have all that I need thank you very much. I am very happy, specially now that Your Majesty has stopped to speak to me."

She laughed softly, touched me on the hand and passed on. They spent twenty minutes with Luang Por and then walked quickly back through the courtyard and were whisked away in their waiting cars to go and inspect the new irrigation system in the valley. I was surrounded by my friends demanding to know what She had said to me and asking how I had been brave enough to reply. In the evening there was to be a big celebration but I was exhausted and asked Tip to take me straight home. Nongnai came to talk to me but her sister, I noticed, did not, nor did I see my brother.

So it is true, This morning I spoke to Chand and asked him point-blank if he had been seeing Tari. He shyly admitted that he had and that he believed she loved him, as he did her. I told him that he should speak to mother and father so that they can approach Tari's parents. He said that he would but that he wanted to wait until after the Flower Festival.

My dear Pan,

Your last letter gave me great joy. Just imagine that you have actually written a story for the newspaper about me and my work! I doubt if they will print it or, even if they do, whether anyone will be in the least interested.

How clever you are! I would never have thought of using carbon paper. Now I will be able to send you a copy of parts of my diary – I certainly will not let you see all of it – without having to write everything twice, but I will have to wait until Tip goes to Chiang Mai as I do not think our local shop stocks carbon paper.

There is love in our house at last, for I can not notice the least trace of love in the marriage of sister Noi and Geow. My brother Chand has fallen in love with the beautiful Tari, one of my best friends. I think she will make Chand very happy and I can not think that her parents will object. My only slight worry is that she has entered the beauty competition at the Flower Festival and Chand, perhaps unwisely, is not going to propose to her until it is over.

I had suspected for sometime that something was going on and this morning I spoke to Chand and he confessed; I pulled his head down to mine and kissed him on the cheek, much to his embarrassment. Apparently he has been afraid to tell anyone, even Tari, of his love, in case he should be rejected as once he was by the *puyai baan*. I told him this was nonsense and that he was good enough for any girl in the village including the precious *puyai baan's* daughter, and that the fortune of our family was now very different from what it had been at that time. Although I am happy, I am sad too, for Chand will go to live with Tari's family; still, it is not far away and it will be lovely to have more nieces and nephews.

This means that there is now room for one more man in this house of ours! Your request for a photograph has had me searching through old papers and dusty cupboards. I have come up with a very complacent, plump little girl of sixteen, standing by the river – I don't think you would like her at all. Then there is the newspaper photograph of a girl lying in hospital looking like a corpse. Next is a photograph, taken only last year, of a girl in a wheelchair with untidy, lank hair and sunken, listless eyes – a hopeless slut and not your type. So I had to go and stare in the looking-glass, something I have not really done for a long, long time. There I saw a thin, pale, rather interesting face with questioning eyes, a face that has suffered, passed through the ordeal and emerged with a new sense of serenity and purpose. I have decided that this girl and no other should send you her photograph. I have written to Mae Khun asking her to bring a camera when next she comes, so you will have to be patient a little while longer. I am still waiting to know how handsome you are, so please hurry and send me your most flattering photograph, but no cheating.

I am not going to tell you about the visit of the King and Queen but rather I enclose a copy of the pages from my diary; this will save me the trouble of having to think what to write all over again, so you see how lazy I really am . Next time I won't even have to write it out twice, will I ?

I wonder what the good points are that you look for in a girl ? My man must work hard, but pretend not to; he must have a sense of humour and also be able to laugh at himself;

he must be as handsome as a film star but not be vain about it; and he must love me madly and only, only me. Do you know anyone like this by any chance ?

I must now get on with my work as, because of all the excitement over the past few days, I have only made twenty-one pieces in the last week, well below my quota of five each day. I would not like you to have it on your conscience that you, too, are stopping me from earning an honest living.

Your affectionate little sister,
Bua Geow

Pan dear,

Your photograph now stands beside me on the table and he often distracts me from my work. At night time he wickedly accompanies me into my bedroom and slips into bed with me to sleep comfortably under my pillow. Sometimes he helps me to sleep peacefully but at other times he keeps me awake for hours thinking about the real man, who has, in this crafty way, come into my life.

But now I must tell you of tragedy in our village. I can accept that ill-fortune comes to one for past misdeeds in a previous life, as it did to me and, perhaps, to you. I find it hard to understand, however, what has befallen Daeng's family. He has never had an easy life; Tari remembers his children at school, although none of them were in her class. Their clothes were often worn and dirty, they seldom had pocket-money even of Fridays and often brought nothing for lunch except sticky rice. Yet they were friendly children and, as far as Tari remembers, did reasonably well. Last year Daeng borrowed money so that he could grow garlic, he lost everything when the river overflowed and washed away his crop.

On Tuesday his daughter, Jane, died; the doctor said she had been bitten by a mosquito with the bleeding disease. Her mother went into shock with grief and died the same evening; the funeral was held on Friday. All the village joined together to buy two cremation towers, which were made at Ban Ap Chang just beyond Mae Rim, one large and one small, painted gold with red decorations. I saw them standing before the house, very splendid, for mother and daughter.

All were assembled for the procession to the crematorium, the monks in robes of saffron, the villagers, in black or white headed by *puyai baan* and the headmaster. Daeng could nowhere be found and the boys, when questioned, said he had not been home all night, so the cremation had to take place without the husband, the father. Daeng's body was found next day in the river.

Pan, can you explain to me what can have brought such a terrible fate to one family ? How did they upset the spirits that they should treat them thus ? They can not surely all have been so evil in a previous life; the coincidence is too great. Wherefore should one family be so punished ? Pan, can you answer me ? The spirts are so unfair. It is lucky only that the three boys are old enough to work, but as they have no close relatives, and as their father has left them nothing but debts, I do not know what will become of them.

Enough of this, I should not burden you with our woes, but I think of you so much that I tell things to you that no one else can know. When I have a new idea or see something of beauty I long to share it with you. I notice that I am even neglecting my diary; you see you have much to answer for.

Because Chand now spends so much time at Tari's or because, perhaps, I am a very different girl this year, I am taking a much more active part in our family affairs. I now keep the money and help decide how it should be used. Anyone who comes to live in this family will find me a hard task-master as I am sure your photograph will already have informed you, for sometimes I think of him as your spy.

Tonight it is very cold, I am warmly wrapped up in bed, but the family is still huddled round a burning log outside. Is it not strange that, although every year it is cold for many days, houses do not have a fire indoors where it would be nice and warm ? Everyone has to crouch round an outside fire that certainly is of no comfort to one's back. Perhaps you should write another story for the newspaper about this.

My body may be a cold but my heart is warm when I think of you, and that is nearly all the time.

Your loving friend,
Bua Keow

This morning Mae Khun came to see me, bringing with her a camera. This put me into such a tizzy of excitement that she must have thought me quite mad. I rushed into my bedroom and called for Tip to come and help me change. I put on the blouse and *pasin* that I was wearing when the Queen spoke to me, although I had promised myself that I would never wear them again until the day I died or, fond hope, the day I married. I wheeled out into the sunlight still brushing my hair and fussing with ribbons. Mae Khun smiled softly and I knew that she had seen into my inner thoughts.

53

"I see you do not want this photograph for your identity card," was all she said. She then took out her lipstick and eyeshadow and insisted on helping me to make myself up, something I has last done in the train on the way to Bangkok.

I tried to look natural, beautiful and intelligent but have no doubt I failed. After our photograph session Mae Khun asked if I would like to visit Pun. Tip helped me into the car, put my chair in the boot and off we drove; I, in all my glory, waved royally to my surprised friends as we passed.

Pun sat like a headmistress, on a bamboo shelf beneath her house, surrounded by six little girls to whom she was teaching cross-stitch work. They were all talking and laughing and the place was covered with coloured cloth and thread. When they saw us, the children scampered off to watch from a safe distance. Pun bubbled with life and Geow stood behind her stiff with pride. Pun produced her finished work from a bag with hilltribe figures embroidered all over it. She had 200 pieces, an average of ten a day, and she has only one eye! Mae Khun looked surprised and, even to me, it was obvious that much of the work had been done by the children. There were many mistakes and Mae Khun told Pun to check them all and re-do the ones that were wrong.

"I am glad that the children are helping you but you must make certain that they do it right," was all she said.

Pun's house is very old, the roof leaks and there are holes in the walls; it is owned by Geow's family and they want to sell the land, so they are trying to force Geow and Pun out, but they have nowhere else to go. The house is quite unsuitable for her as, although she can move quite well on the stumps of her legs, it is painful to watch her climbing the steep steps up to the house and even worse to watch her coming down again. Mae Khun asked Pun if

54

there was any place where they could build themselves a new house. Pun said she thought her mother would let them build a small house on her land; Mae Khun told her to find out and they would talk about it next time for, she said, there was a profit of over Bts. 20,000 from the cards we had sold so far, which could be used. I was very glad to see Pun looking well and clearly enjoying herself teaching the children. She was a very different person from the one Tari described after she had visited her only a few weeks before. How much a new interest in life, a sense of being needed again, can do for someone who has given up.

I have not, I realise, written about the Flower Festival which is surprising since it has been preoccupying the village for months past, even though our family has not been directly involved. Every year in February, just at the end of the cold season, there is a great Festival in Chiang Mai. This is the time when winter flowers are at their best and Suan Buak Hard, the city park, is ablaze with holly-hocks, salvia, forget-me-nots, petunia and marigolds. All the nurseries vie with each other to grow larger and more exotic flowers, and there are competitions on the day of the Festival with special classes for orchids, roses, arrangements, new varieties and so on. The main attraction, however, is the procession of floral floats that passes through the beflagged streets from the University to the Park. Each large village such as Doi Saket, Mae Rim and Sankampaeng, each important establishment such as the University, Thai International and the Chiang Inn Hotel, designs a float depicting a garuda, a peacock, a *chedi* or some such thing and decorates it with massed flowers, Sitting atop will be a beauty queen surrounded by her maidens. In the evening a beauty contest is held to choose Miss Chiang Mai who then goes on to enter the Miss Thailand competition.

This year, for the first time, our village had decided to enter. This has resulted in a tremendous amount of work and argument, for money has had to be raised, flowers grown, a truck borrowed and the design agreed upon. All that is now behind us, thank goodness. Each family was asked to give twenty baht some more if it was felt that they could afford it, seeds of asters and marigolds were bought and planted; See the rice mill owner, has lent his truck free of charge, believe it or not; and the headmaster and his staff have turned it into a royal swan made out of foam plastic. It now stands in a shed behind the school, white and naked, waiting for the flowers that will be stuck onto it next week. Mother and her friends will have yet another happy but sleepless night, for the flowers will only be put on at the very last moment to make certain they do not wilt during the procession.

The other burning issue is the selection of our beauty queen. After much debate a special committee has been set up to do this onerous task. Six good men and true led by *puyai baan* and including the headmaster, See, because he lent his truck and, I do not know why, father. They put up notices inviting girls to send in their names and approached the fathers of girls they themselves fancied. From all these applicants twelve have been invited to go to the school this evening and from among them will be chosen Miss Mae Taeng.

In its wisdom the committee has prepared a check list to help in the judgement. Up to ten points are to be awarded for each of seven attributes; the girl who receives the greatest number of points when all are added up will win. These are the qualities of beauty they have chosen:

Hair, face, shape, intelligence, movement, feet, bottom.

How this list was arrived at, I know not, but I suppose it is as likely to produce the right result as any other. Father says intelligence will be judged by asking each girl three questions (I have promised not to tell anyone what they are). "What will you do if you become Miss Chiang Mai ?" "Name three varieties of garlic." "Who is the Prime Minister of Thailand ?"

Poor Chand is distraught, he does not know if he should be glad or miserable, for all the village gamblers are betting heavily that Tari will win. He has now disappeared and I expect will be watching the contest from some hidden and solitary spot. Father has already bustled off with his sheaf of judgement papers, weighed down by them and his great responsibility.

Tip and Nongnai had pushed me through the village to the school. The last part was hard work as the lane is uphill and sandy so the little front wheels of my chair kept digging in and I was nearly thrown out. Finally they had to turn me round and pull me backwards up the lane.

The main school building is on the slope of a hill and several steps lead up from the football field to a large terrace before the main entrance. It was there, in front of the flag staff, on which I was surprised to see the flag still flying even though it was nearly dark, that the judges sat. Seven solemn men behind a green-topped table strewn with papers, pencils and glasses of water; flood-lights shone down for, on the space in front of them, the girls were to parade. The seventh man turned out to be the owner of Chiang Mai Muang Dek, a shop in Chiang Mai selling toys and teenage clothes, who had agreed to sponsor the winner in the Miss Chiang Mai contest. All the young men of the village, some of whom already had had too much to drink, clustered round the bottom of the steps talking noisily and cheering any of the contestants they happened to see.

Puyai baan banged on the table with his glass spilling water all over father's papers and when the noise had died down, he explained that each girl in turn would come out from the door behind him, walk twice past the judges and then go down the steps into the waiting crowd. Finally all the girls would come back and stand before the judges while the points were added up and the winner and runner-up chosen.

Luk Tung music crackled from the old loudspeakers as the first girl tripped out into the glare of the lights. I did not know her well. She had obviously gone to a lot of trouble over her hair which was piled high like a straw-stack and festooned with bangles – ten points for certain, I thought.

The face was a failure, she had covered it with make-up and the result was a disaster. Shape, if all genuine, was quite good. Movement, well, she had not fallen over yet. I had been puzzling over how they would judge her feet, but now she stopped in front of the judges, jerked her *pasin* up above her knee and placed first one bare foot and then the other on a box that I had not noticed standing in front of the judges; they all had to lean forward to be able to see her feet over the edge of the table. It was while she was in this rather ridiculous position that *puyai baan* asked the questions to test her intelligence. Nongnai, who knows her well, whispered that her score for this should be zero. She then turned her back on the judges and wobbled perilously down the steps so that only they could fairly give points to her last attribute, 'the bottom'. She fled from the circle of cheering youths and joined her friends somewhere in the dark.

All the girls wore Thai costume, most had elaborate hair styles, and too much make-up. Number Five was a disaster from start to finish; her name was Add, the youngest daughter of See, the rice mill owner, and I suspect he had only agreed to lend his truck on condition that she appeared in the final selection, for I can think of no other reason for her presence. She turned the wrong way as she came out of the door and had to be redirected, her hair came undone and in an effort to put it right she managed only to smear lipstick all over her cheek. Our laughter turned to sympathy as she slipped on the steps and bounced down on her bottom, the only part of her body that might, conceivably, have earned her some points.

"Tammatari! Tammatari Kampong! *Puyai baan* called out. Strangely, I had never known that this was her full name.

Her hair hung loose, she wore no make-up, save a slash of crimson lipstick. She was in white with a golden *sabai* across her chest. She came to the front and made a *wai* first to the judges, and then to us. With great poise she walked slowly back and forth; disdainfully she placed each foot on the box without raising her *pasin*, she stepped back before answering the questions, then turned and floated down the steps without once lowering her eyes. The applause was deafening and genuine; the rest of the girls, we all felt, need not bother to come out and the judges need not add up their points. We all wanted there and then to acclaim Tari, Miss Mae Taeng, Miss Chiang Mai, Miss Universe.

But the show went on; even when the girls stood awkwardly waiting for the points to be added up, Tari stood out like one lighted candle amongst eleven that had never been lit. When the golden paper crown was placed on her head it seemed to belong there. Tari stepped forward, held up her hand and silence fell.

"I thank you all," she said softly, yet her voice carried as clearly as reflected moonlight across a river.*

She stepped back and her friends rushed up to congratulate her, all that is except for Chand. She was neither proud nor shy; this was a part she was born to play; she looked a beauty queen and now quite naturally she acted like one and my heart sank for poor Chand. Could he

---

* Some there were present that night, who thought she then said:

"Now that I have been chosen, and now that the Seal has been refound I am ready to bear the burden of Tammatari and, through me, Chamadevi's spirit will once again give hope to the weak and strength to the brave."

But maybe it was not so.

60

aspire to this new Tari ? She did not come home with us for she had to make arrangements with her sponsor from Chiang Mai; again I thought how well she got into his white Mercedes. No one could have guessed that she had never been in a saloon car before in her life. She is a strange girl. Sometimes she frightens me. She was never meant to be born in Mae Taeng, I think.

We have just finished a family meeting to which even Noi and Geow came, for we had a difficult decision to make concerning our garlic. I seem to spend a great deal of time writing about garlic. If anyone ever reads this diary he will, no doubt, smell it on every page. It is of so much importance to us. Rice keeps us alive, but all our little luxuries come from garlic; the success or failure of the crop makes the difference between a harsh year of want and a good year of prosperity.

Yesterday a merchant fromm Chiang Mai came to look at our fields and has offered to buy the entire crop, except for the one *rai* we have fertilized with buffalo manure instead of chemicals and which we will keep for next year's seed, for ten baht a kilo. We would harvest the crop which he would then weigh and take away in his trucks. The problem is that today's price is twelve baht a kilo and our crop will not be ready for another two weeks. Father and Chand believe that the price will go up so that we should not selll to this man. I think that, in two weeks time, the price will have fallen to eight baht and that we should sell.

I have watched foreign films in which members of a family argue, contradict and shout at each other and yet end up in agreement and the best of friends. Our customs are different; we listen to, and usually obey, those who are older than ourselves; even when we know they are wrong and stupid, we do not argue or contradict them; we do not like open confrontation, perhaps because village life is so public. If someone upsets or insults us we turn and walk away; furious inside and no doubt plotting revenge, but saying nothing. We find it difficult to discuss matters or argue about a problem and reach a compromise. I remember the silly affair over where to plant a *lamyai* tree. Father wanted it at the front of the house, Mother at the back; it was finally left to die unplanted. When a government official orders us to do something, we will say 'yes' but that can mean. "Yes, I heard what you said, I agree with you and I will do it." "Yes, I heard what you said, you may be right but I won't do it". Or. "Yes, I heard what you said, I don't agree with you and I won't do it."

Chand started by saying that we should not sell because we could not trust the merchant. "He will certainly use scales that understate the weight of our garlic." Father quickly agreed as this was a good reason for not selling the garlic and yet had nothing to do with the real issue of price. "That is easily solved," I said. "We can buy our own scales, have them checked by a government official and insist that everything is also weighed on our scales." There was now a direct confrontation between Chand and myself, for the others refused to enter the argument. Chand had been in a foul mood ever since the beauty contest as he felt he was loosing Tari and he had been finding fault with everyone and everything. This made him an unpleasant but a weak adversary as I now told him. He walked out in a temper and I was left the victor. This is not nice as I now have the great worry of having forced a decision that may be wrong. I am going to leave a space here in my diary that I will fill up in two weeks time; I shall simply say what the market price is then.

(The market price is Bts. 7.50. Hooray!)

Whilst still on the subject of garlic, I recall that one of the first things I ever wrote about in this, my diary, was Chand's refusal to lend our water pump to uncle Put. That story has now ended badly. After Chand's refusal, Put went to a money lender and borrowed Bts. 5,000 at 10% interest a month. As security he gave the title deeds of his fields and also the land on which his house stands. He signed an agreement that, if he could not repay the loan when he harvested his garlic he would forfeit all his security and the water pump. Put bought the pump, planted his garlic and covered it with straw, but he did not have any money left with which to buy fertilizer. Last week he harvested his crop, while the money-lender watched from his car. The heads of garlic were so small that his yield was only a third of ours and the quality so poor that he only got three baht a kilo. He received Bts. 4,500 for his total crop. The money-lender, who was hoping for this, immediately seized all his land and poor Put has left the village. We hear that he has gone to live with distant relatives who have some rice fields near Chiang Dow. It is lucky he never married.

My dear Pan,

Enclosed is a photograph of the girl in the looking-glass. I am so afraid that, now you have seen what the girl who writes those silly letters to you looks like, I will never hear from you again. I did, however, introduce her to your photograph and he did not disapprove.

You ask if I can write poetry. Of course not! Who do you think I am, some over-educated scholar like Por Khun? Yours, though, is just beautiful; I can see myself as the Princess you tell of, directing the happiness of the world from her mountain top, but I think I shall need you to help me as there is so much sorrow waiting to be changed, as by your alchemist, into golden pleasure.

Tomorrow I am to be taken to Chiang Mai to watch the Flower Festival. Mae Khun has arranged for me to go to Chiang Mai Muang Dek since she knows the owner who is sponsoring Tari. The procession goes right past the shop. The village is in a flurry of excitement; the flowers have all been cut and put in deep water to soak, this afternoon all the school children will help cut the stalks off and sort the flowers into colour and size, and this evening mother's group will start decorating the float which has to be in

Chiang Mai all ready by eight o'clock tomorrow morning.

Tari is here today but goes back to Chiang Mai this afternoon to start getting ready. I have never seen her look so vivacious, she seems to glow from within. You should have used her as the model for your Princess for she behaves like one more and more every day as if she were playing a part that she had played before. It is very strange. She now has many beautiful clothes including a swimming costume that would shock the village elders. On the day of the contest she will have a team of hairdressers, make-up artists and dressmakers who will follow her every step, patching up and repairing as necessary.

I am so excited about tomorrow that I feel a little sick as if it was I who was taking part in the procession. I therefore send this letter as a wrapper for that girl's photograph since that is the only thing in it of any interest. I promise to write at length once I have recovered from the effects of tomorrow.

Your mountain Princess sends you all happiness.

Bua Geow

Three days have passed since the Festival and only now am I able to pick up my pen again. I have been completely exhausted and spent with an overdose of excitement; let me start at end. She was superb, breathtakingly beautiful, the girl was born to be a Queen and we never knew it. Yes, our Tari is now Miss Chiang Mai. From the first moment she stepped onto the stage there was no doubt but that she would win.

A sudden hush, a collective catching-in-of-breath, and then spontaneous applause showed the verdict of the audience. Tammatari responded as, if you will forgive a Mae Taeng expression, garlic does to manure; she loved everything and everyone, the audience, the judges, the cameras, she took them into her arms, as it were, and loved them with her eyes and they could not help but love her in return.

First she appeared, almost as she had at Mae Taeng, all in white silk with a golden *sabai*, her hair loose and long. But now she also wore jewellery – earrings, a necklace and rings – while skillfully applied make-up seemed somehow to brighten her eyes. Next she came in her swimming costume, her hair piled up in the style of Apasara, and she wore heavy make-up, bright scarlet lipstick and darkly smudged eyes; she shocked us with her savage beauty. I had never seen so much of her exposed and I marvelled that she, who had spent so many hours toiling in the sun of the fields, could be such a perfect vision of fairness. Finally the girls stepped out in their European evening gowns, each more ornate and decorative than the last, a procession of dazzling crimsons, purples and golds, of lace and frills all topped with made-up faces and pyramid hairdos. Tari had no make-up, her hair swung free and she wore a simple, tight fitting black dress cut alarmingly low in the front. In her cleavage, on its chain of gold, hung a pendant that looked like an elephant. The effect, the contrast, was overwhelming; once again came that collective intake of breath followed by applause that would not stop, for everyone knew that before them stood not only the new Miss Chiang Mai but the future Miss Thailand.

The first surprise of the day had been the wife of Tari's sponsor, very beautiful and vaguely familiar. It was only when Mae Khun joined us on the balcony that I saw the resemblance, for this was her younger sister. Once again she had been quietly at work behind the scene arranging a sponsor for our beauty queen. Por Khun was there as pompous as ever and I realised, with a twinge of remorse, that I had not thought of him for a long time, but nor, for that matter, had he been to see me. There was also a handsome if rather overweight man in his late twenties whom everyone call Ajarn. A group of noisy children, cousins and friends of Mae Khun's daughter, Pim, had come to watch her riding a horse in the procession. Apparently she practices every weekend with the Pack Squadron at Mae Rim.

At eleven o'clock we heard music in the distance and the crowd below us rippled in expectation, like a dog shaking its coat; children ran onto the road and had to be called back by anxious parents, cameras were readied and food stowed away. Round the corner marched the band of Monfort College, smartly dressed in red and white, playing a tune written by the King; next came troops of boy scouts and girl guides; then the first float from Doi Saket. It was a beautiful grass-covered mountain on which grew yellow chrysanthemums and arum lilies, intermixed with sprays of orchids. At the back was a peacock, its green tail, made from fronds, spread wide; sitting on the peacock's back, shaded by a red parasol, was Miss Doi Saket. She wore an orange costume and a green *sabai*; her smile, after riding her peacock for an hour through the heat of the day, was strained and her make-up had run, but she was brave and pretty. Then in succession came a pink and white replica of a famous Lampun *chedi*, a purple and gold garuda and a yellow elephant; more music from the girls band of Regina College; a rattle of hooves and six horses rounded the corner led by Pim bearing the national flag. The bridles and saddle-cloths of the horses were embroidered with red and white carnations and each had a plume of orchids on its head, small bells jingling as they moved. Suddenly, just below us, a ballon burst. Pim's horse reared up but she controlled and soothed it; the boy behind lost his seat and fell heavily to the road but he managed to keep hold of the reins of the plunging horse which otherwise would have bolted into the crowd. Shaken, but not badly hurt, the boy bravely mounted again and they rode on in good order.

The procession flowed past before our eyes, floats of flowers and beautiful girls interspersed with people marching, children on bicycles and roller-skates, girls in samlors peddling past, a group of Thai-style boxers in their red and blue robes, soldiers stiff and in time, even three elephants with girls swaying dangerously in the howdahs. Almost at the very end came Mae Taeng. We had done well for a first effort. Our swan looked very royal, even if his neck hung down a little, even if the flowers had wilted after so long a wait in the sun, but the neck of Miss Mae Taeng did not hang down nor had she wilted. The crowd was beginning to drift away after a long day but something seemed to stop them now and they turned back to look. I very much doubt if anyone noticed our float, all eyes were on Tammatari. I do not know what had happened to her or how she did it but she seemed to look straight into the eyes of every man, woman, and child, and send a personal message of love, especially to the women. Her smile was not strained, she looked radiant and knew it; this was her day and she was joyously sharing it with her devotees.

After she had passed, raising her left eyebrow in that quizzical way of hers and waving to us as she went, there was a moment of awed silence.

"She's a winner!" cried Ajarn jumping to his feet. "This calls for celebration, she had the crowd in her pocket, we will have to start thinking about how to sponsor her for Miss Thailand!" He produced a bottle of champagne as if he had known all the time how well Tari would look, and perhaps he had for he obviously gave much attention to the study of beauty, but then perhaps he always drank champagne in the afternoon, too. He was not an Ajarn at the University as I had thought but the owner of Gloria, a famous cosmetic company, an extremely rich and accomplished ladies' man and a bachelor. If this man was to be her future sponsor poor Chand could say farewell to his lost love. He had missed his chance by waiting to propose until after the Festival, for this new Tammatari had grown wings and would never again accept the humdrum life of a village. Perhaps Chand had felt something of this and had known that, even if she had accepted his proposal two weeks ago, for she surely loved him then, he could never have held her. It was funny, I thought, how often Tari now spoke of herself as Tammatari as if she was some different and rather special person, not to be confused with the naive Tari of Mae Taeng.

Ajarn insisted that everyone, including me, should drink to the success of Tari. "To she who is already Miss Chiang Mai," (although she was not) " and to the future Miss Thailand," he called. I knew he was carefully working out how he could fit her into his personal life and how he could use her to promote his cosmetics. Now I can not drink, yet in the excitement of the moment I finished my glass! Within minutes I had gone bright red. I could feel my

69

skin burning round my neck and over my breasts, voices spun far away and the room rocked from side to side. I slept for four hours and fortunately recovered in time to go to the Beauty Competition that I have already described.

Hot winds are blowing down the valley and for much of the time smoke haze hides the mountains. Now all is dry, the grass brown and the winter flowers over. Last night fires burned on the mountain side, one in the shape of a letter T moved rapidly before the wind eating up the dead leaves, the low growing grasses and plants then occasionally shooting upwards as a clump of bamboos or a tree turned into a torch. It is sad to see this annual destruction of the forests. Some fires are accidental, started, maybe, by a piece of glass caught in the rays of the sun or by the careless cigarette of a tourist, but more often it is the hilltribe people who fire the slopes to prepare the ground for their new crop of rice or opium, for slash-and-burn cultivation is all they know. Also, when the new grass springs up after the fire, animals come to feed and they are easily able to kill them.

Now is the time of year, March, when a heavy heat settles into the valley filling it with the sweet scent of *lamyai* blossom. We are all listless from this heat. Even the flame trees seem to have given up; they have dropped their leaves, their branches look dried and dead; yet within weeks they will have burst into glorious scarlet blossom just in time for Songkram. We begin now to think ahead to Songkram, the new year and the rains that will come, the ploughing and the backache of rice planting. And I? I think of Pan and that I am soon to meet him for the first time. Is it a mistake, I wonder? We have revealed so much to each other of ourselves, our beliefs, thoughts and hopes. Should we go on, lovers by letter, or take the risk of meeting, the risk that the looking-glass will break, the girl with it? But somehow I think it will work, so does Mae Khun who is arranging for us to meet at her house on Monday.

71

Pan, my darling,

So we are to meet at last, the girl in the lookin- glass and the spy who sleeps under my pillow. Whatever happens, my world will never be the same again. I feel like a small girl who has just been given a box containing, she is told, the doll she has always dreamed of owning but has known she never would. Should she go on dreaming of her lovely doll or should she risk opening the box only to find that the doll is not at all what she had imagined it to be ?

You ask me how I pass my days. Well, I am, as you know, a lazy person, so I get up at seven o'clock. If there is no one at home, which is usually the case, I spend a long time washing and dressing myself even though it is not difficult for me to decide what to wear, since I only have three blouses and *pasin* to choose from. Ribbons are much more of a problem but I have already told you that I have a thing about them. I usually choose the correct colour for the day of the week: Monday, yellow; Tuesday, pink; Wednesday, green; Thursday, orange; Friday, blue; Saturday, purple; Sunday, red. This saves me having to make a decision. Next I have breakfast which Tip will have left on the table for me. If we can afford it, I have a glass of Ovaltine with my sticky rice, fried vegetables and chilli paste. Then comes the time for household chores, nothing much, mind you; I may wash some of my clothes, or Tip's and mother's if they are busy. I tidy my room as well as I am able and then go to see if anything needs doing outside. I check that the pigs and chickens have been fed, talk to the dogs and water the flowers and herbs, unless it happens to be raining.

It is now mid-morning and I work at my cross-stitch figures until lunchtime. Sometimes Dam and Nit come to play around me and I try to teach them reading and writing, or I tell them stories or let them play at sewing. Usually someone will come home to share my mid-day meal; I do not have to tell you what I eat for I am sure you eat the same – certainly you will have to if ever you come and visit us. Heavy with sticky rice I go to lie down, and perhaps sleep, through the heat of the day.

At about four o'clock I come out refreshed, finish my quota of sewing, if it has not been done, and then wait for the family to drift home tired and dirty from their day's work. We eat supper together, sticky rice, vegetable soup, fried vegetables, some meat, and perhaps curry, rich in garlic, followed by fruit. Friends may come round to chat in the evening cool or Tip will push me out to visit Nongnai or other friends nearby. Everyone goes to bed early except for me who will sit for another hour or so writing my diary or a letter to you until I, too, feel tired and fall onto my bed to dream of you. Do you dream ? I do and in colour, but I shall not tell you of what.

Sweet dreams, my love,
Bua Geow

The money we got from our garlic crop was more than we had dared to hope, for our yield was one of the highest in the valley. My small family victory over the price at which we should sell, has given us Bts, 8,000 more than we would otherwise have made. But it is a hollow victory, for poor Chand has left home heart-broken over Tari, the second lost love of his life. Our joke that we would buy him a bride with our profits has fallen very flat. All else we promised ourselves that evening, we have now bought. I have my television set, a colour one too! Tip has her Honda motorbike, my parents their new clothes, the babies their toys and money will still be left over even after we have built the barn.

We have not heard from Chand since the day after the Flower Festival but we believe he is working on a building site in Chiang Mai. I pray that he will wash her out of his life and come back to us at Songkram. It will be hard for him to forget Tari though, for often her photograph is in the newspapers and her face on television. We see her opening a new shop, giving presents, usually Gloria cosmetics, to sick people, orphans or old age pensioners who are scarcely likely to want them, or she is attending a grand party in aid of some charity or other – now that I have my television I am constantly surprised to see how much people eat for charity; we see her shaking hands with foreigners and I am told she has invented a handshake so sexy that men insist on coming back for another one – it is something to do with the way she presses her thumb on the back of their hand, the gossip columnists tell us. It is sad that she has not once been back to see her parents since she won her title, but her sponsors seem to be making use of her a great deal.

Pun's house, I hear, is growing apace. Since it is right on the lane it has been decided that she will run it as a shop. It will cost about Bts. 25,000 to build. Pun will give all the money she makes from her work; Geow will be responsible for finding the wood in the forest and cutting it into planks, the rest will be paid for by Mae Khun or rather by all of us. Over 10,000 cards have been sold since we started work last year and the profit after all expenses, is Bts. 21,000. This money will be used to build Pun's shop; it is good to think that we have all been able to help her in this way.

My Pan,

This may well be the last letter I shall ever write to you, for on Monday we meet. From what you have written, if I have understood correctly, you like the girl in the looking-glass and I for my part, have fallen in love with my spy. What then can our next step be ? Let us be sensible. We are not as other people, and yet are we so very different ? In that magazine you sent me about the handicapped people of Thailand – can there really be as many as seven hundred thousand of us, nearly as many as the total population of Chiang Mai ? – there was a lovely story about two young people who fell in love during an archery match for the disabled: they married and lived happily together. Why have you not written for that magazine ? Even its name *chavit wan nee.* It is so wonderful. Shall I, do you think, send them a copy of my diary?

Consider seriously what we should say to each other when we meet face to face on Monday. I already know what I shall reply to you, if you say what I hope you will – so be warned!

You asked me to write a poem; since this may be my last letter I had better set it down. Please burn it before reading.

Oh! the joy that you feel
Is to me as a tune,
As a toy to a child,
As a song to the moon.

Whilst the grief that you meet
Is to me as a pain
I would fain bear for you,
Though I die of that grief.

75

So then live to the full,
While your youth is yet pure;
In the year of your death
You may pray and forgive.

But not now is the time
To sleep in the spring
Or to bow to the gods
Or to kneel - but to sing.

But to sing to the sky
And to shout o'er the sea
And to bring to the world
The thrill that we feel to will and to be.

Bua Geow

Meow came to see me yesterday. I have not mentioned her before, but then she is not the sort of girl that anyone ever notices. This is her story.

"My mother ran away when I was three and has not been heard of since. I gather she did not know who my father was, for she had many customers. I was brought up by my grandmother. You have probably not seen our house which squats on a marshy piece of ground behind the crematorium. The roof is made of leaves which keep us dry enough, as long as it does not rain. The walls are a patchwork of rusty tins, beaten flat, and cardboard boxes that have to be replaced every few months. We have no lavatory but the holes in the floor make a useful exit for all sorts of refuse. There are only two rooms in the house.

"My grandmother, who seems always to have been alone, ekes out a living by collecting old bottles, paper and other odds and ends which she sells to a merchant who calls once a month. She scavenges a little for food and has an understanding with the village store that they will supply her free with tobacco for the long cigars she makes herself, rolled into banana leaves. Every day she goes into the forest and usually comes home with something to eat with our rice. Bamboo shoots, edible fungus, leaves and creepers, berries, sometimes, I don't know how, a small bird or animal, and often insects or maggots.

"I never went to school and from the age of eight earned a few baht a day carrying water from the river. You may have seen me climbing up the bank and going along the lane to one house or another with my two cans hanging from a pole over my shoulders. I hardly spilt a drop and I came to enjoy the rhythm of my walk. I was still doing this, for it was all I knew, when I was fifteen. I wore my only *pasin*, grandmother had found it some years before, and my top

77

was partly concealed by a rag held together in places with pieces of string.

"I was a wild creature, untamed and untouchable. Yet, I now realise, my very wildness was erotic; my hair swung over my face, my breasts often showed clearly through my rags and my *pasin* slid right up my thigh when I climbed the river bank. My business was water so I was always clean, I swam in the river every day and that was my greatest joy. The youths of the village started to come and watch me, some even tried to speak to me but I did not know what it was all about.

"One day grandmother told me that See's son wanted to marry me. He was one of the youths I had noticed. Apparently See was furious as he had already planned a very good match for his son, whose name was Won, with the schoolmaster's ugly daughter. Won was disowned and the next day he moved into our house. We did not bother to register our marriage, Won simply gave me a new *pasin* and grandmother five hundred baht. The first night I went to sleep with grandmother as usual in the small room and I assumed Won would sleep on his mat in the big room. I was therefore surprised when he called to me after a short while and beckoned me to join him where he lay. I knelt beside him and he immediately grabbed me and tried to undo my *pasin*. Terrified I tore myself away leaving it in his groping hands and fled, naked, back to my grandmother.

"Next morning I told Won I was ill, refused to get up, and asked him to go and fetch some medicine for me. For four days I lay there pretending to be ill, eating little and having to swallow the foul medicine they brought for me.

"My grandmother had never told me anything about life. I knew nothing of sex, I just felt a great fear of this unknown Won who had tried to grab me. On the fifth day he went out with his friends, who must have told him that

I was faking illness and that he would have to use force. He returned noisily drunk, came into our room and pulled me up. I did not dare to fight for fear of disturbing grandmother. He hurt me that night and still I did not know what it was all about.

"I never slept with him again although I put a mattress in the outside room and lay near him. Then my period did not come and I felt sick in the morning – I was afraid that I had caught some disease from him. There was no one I could talk to, for neither grandmother nor I had any friends. One day as I was carrying water into *puyai baan's* house I fainted. So it was that I learned I was pregnant.

"When he heard the news Won decided that his father's choice of the schoolmaster's ugly daughter had been right and he told me he was leaving. Looking back I can hardly blame him. If only he had explained to me what it was all about, but then how could he have imagined that anyone could be so totally ignorant as I was ? The midwife called on See and told him that he should at least give some money to cover the expense of his grandson's birth. He gave us what I, in my naivety, thought was a fortune, a thousand baht.

"Won came to collect his things. He did not say sorry or goodbye but he promised that he would collect fuel himself for my birth-fire and bring it to me after the child was born. I told him I never wanted to see him or his fuel again and that I would rather have no fire than one made from wood of his.

"My girl is now six months old, I still live with my grandmother. We owe money to the midwife that can never be repaid, for a thousand baht was not enough. I am sixteen years old. Bua Geow, is there anything I can do besides carry water, do you think ?"

There and then I made Meow sit down beside me. I gave her some material, a needle and thread and our lessons began.

Pan, oh Pan, my love

It was all right, wasn't it ?

There sat I under the lynchee tree on the lawn of Mae Khun's house pretending to be doing my cross-stitch work, but in truth anxiously watching the door for you to come out, for I had heard the car. Suddenly you were there, wheeling alone across the lawn from the other direction. What a dirty trick to steal up on a poor girl so! We laughed with each other from afar and we knew one another so well that there was never an awkward moment, never that embarrassment of a first meeting. I said "When are you coming?" and you said "At Songkram." So we were engaged this day.

We talked a little together, do you remember ? Then I called out and Por Khun, Mae Khun and Pim, Pim walking on her stilts, came to us. They knew at once that all was well. You said, do you remember ? that you would have to ask my father's permission to marry me and I said that you need not, for he had already given it. You then pulled a small box out of your pocket, took out the ring and put it on my finger. It fitted perfectly – I wonder why ?

We talked and laughed as if we had been always together. Lunch on the lawn, Pim eating hers over our heads in her treehouse; love songs from a wireless in a nearby house, the heavy fragrance of *lamyai* blossom and the chirping of birds in the trees. Do you remember all this, Pan ? I went home in the afternoon and we have been talking ever since about the changes we will make to the house before you arrive.

Your loving wife-to-be,
Bua Geow

What wonderful news! Yesterday a big car came cautiously up the lane. One of the two ladies who got out was the Queen's lady-in-waiting who had made notes about our work on the day when the Queen spoke to me. She asked to see all the different designs that we made, so I showed her the four hilltribe figures, the little boys, the bears, the Father Christmases and the Thai International logo. She asked about the Thai International one and I explained that this had been Por Khun's idea. He had sent samples to the manager and had been very angry when no one had even bothered to reply. The lady, whom the Queen had called Thongtip, and who, I now discovered, was a Khunying, said she would find out what had happened for she thought Thai International should certainly buy from us.

She then ordered two thousand pieces of various designs to be made up in our standard cards for the Chitralada shops and five thousand pieces, all hilltribes, that the Queen would have made up herself. This is wonderful! It means that, with the orders we already have, twenty girls can now work for the rest of the year. Pun's house can be finished and Mae Khun will be able to help other disabled girls to live a good life. Khunying Thongtip promised to come and see me again soon and I asked her also to visit Pun, whose house, I hear, is nearly finished.

I have done no cross-stitch work for many days; life has been too busy and my thoughts have been elsewhere. We have decided to have a grand wedding in Chiang Mai, not a northern village wedding at all but a Bangkok style affair complete with a reception. We are doing this, not because either of us wants to, but because we both feel it will serve as an example of hope and encouragement to the thousands of disabled people who have not had the chance to overcome the crushing of their body and their spirit that we have had.

Although the wedding will be very expensive, friends and supporters of our Charity are paying for everything. Tari's sponsors, Ajarn and Wiwat, will provide the cake and drinks, Mae Khun and some of her friends, who have helped to sell our cards, will make the food, and Khunying Thongtip will send some flower arrangements made in the Palace at Bangkok. I will feel so very lost and small because this is not at all the kind of wedding for a poor village girl, but after all, Pan's family does come from Bangkok.

The very first thing I did after our engagement was to go with mother to see Luang Por. All my old fears over not knowing the date of my birth came flooding back. What if my star could not live with that of Pan ? He had already given me his horoscope but how could mine be told ? What if we could not marry after all ? I recalled the story of Somboon who fell in love and went to ask on what day he should marry, only to be told that if he wed this girl his mother would die. He did not believe what had been said to him and went to a fortune-teller in Chiang Mai, who told him exactly the same thing. He has never married even though his mother has long since died.

There was, too, the fact that my older brother and one of my older sisters were not yet married.

Luang Por spends most of his time in his own *kuti* at the back of the *wat* grounds. It is a little house with a verandah, surrounded by carefully tended flower beds and shaded by great mango trees. My chair had to be lifted up and I was then pushed into the room where he sat half reclining on a couch. Mother entered on her knees and made the traditional three gestures of respect, her hands above her head, her forehead touching the floor; I could only *wai*.

It was a crowded room but comfortable. On the altar were many beautiful figures of the Lord Buddha. One I noticed in particular was a golden walking statue that smiled gently and seemed to glide towards me; flowers in vases, incense sticks and candles stood on the altar table. On the walls were many pictures telling some of the Jataka stories, and also two photographs of the King and Queen giving robes to Luang Por at Katin. Piled on the floor were vases, books, boxes of candles, soap and detergent, dried flowers, tins of food and cushions, gifts that had been brought to him by his many visitors. Beside Luang Por sat Pra Noi who looks after his wants.

Although Luang Por's mind is still as clear as January sky at night, he is extremely deaf and only Pra Noi is able to make himself understood, so all questions pass through him but the answers come back direct, which is sometimes rather disconcerting. Mother said that I was going to be married, placed Pan's horoscope on the floor in front of Pra Noi and then explained that she did not know my date of birth or the time, although it must have been early in the morning as the cocks were crowing. I added that I was also worried because Chand and Tip were still single. With a gesture of his hand Luang Por dismissed all this as being of no importance and called me to come closer. He prayed silently and then said. "Your brother will marry soon after you and Tip is not the kind of girl who will marry a man, so do not wait. You two were destined to meet in this life and to marry. The only two days that are right for you are the last of the year or eve of Lent. Your time is nine, nine minutes past two for wedding and nine minutes past four of the evening for bedding. You deserve to be happy, my child. Now go, I am tired. Go, go child and be happy."

Elated, I wrote to Pan and Mae Khun telling then the news. Pan will indeed be here for Songkram. All the arrangements are up to them now, there is little I can do but wait and supervise the alterations and decoration of our downstairs rooms.

Meow has proved to be a sweet girl, quick to learn and really as innocent as she sounded in her story. She comes and sits with me every day and does her cross-stitch work fast and neatly while talking amusing nonsense at the same time. She knows a great deal about everyone in the village for she was totally ignored as she went in and out of the houses with her water, and so heard and saw much that no one else ever knew. We have fixed up a cradle for her baby who is called Luk Nam. It hangs from the roof beam like a hammock and Meow pulls it with a rope, gently rocking the baby every few minutes, as she sings *"Noi, noi, noi noi noi noi"*

Yesterday a thin and silent Chand returned. He has told us nothing of where he has been or what he has done. Apparently he wants to become a monk as soon as possible, but has reluctantly agreed to wait until after our wedding. I pray that he will be able to forget Tari, for we all agree that she is now far too grand ever to be able to come back to Mae Taeng.

I hear reports of great preparations for the twelfth of next month; invitations have been sent out to all our relations and to our friends in the village. Everything is unreal to me, this time of my engagement is somehow like a false dawn, the cock has crowed but dawn has not followed. I worry that marriage may not work for us, for we have met but once.

I have not opened my diary for over a month. Reading over the last few pages. I notice that they are scrappy and poorly written and perhaps this reflects my mood at that time. I was not to see Pan again until our wedding day, nor did he write to me except on matters of business. He went to stay at Mae Khun's house so that they could work together on the preparations, and I came to resent the fact that the two of them were scheming behind my back, making all the arrangements without ever consulting me, as if I was of no importance, as if the wedding was of no importance except as a form of promotion of the Bua Geow Charity for such was the official name that had now been given to our cross-stitch work.

At last the day came, the day before The Day. I packed the new clothes I had bought, the *pasin* and blouse I had worn before the Queen and for my photograph, and a selection of ribbons, neatly into four large plastic bags. Por Khun fetched me in the afternoon, for I was to stay at their house for two nights, the first night alone, for Pan had moved out to stay with friends, the second night with my husband.

I heard the cocks crow the false dawn in, I was up and dressed before they crowed again and lightness came to the world; Pan arrive before the sun. The previous day Tip, mother and I had prepared enough food to give to nine monks, *gaeng hoh*, *naem* and sticky rice in individual plastic bags, coconut *kanom* wrapped in banana leaves that Noi had made, cigarettes and *miang*, for Pan and I had decided that we would go alone, at break of day and make merit on our wedding day by giving food to the monks. We went to the road that runs beside the irrigation canal and sat there together holding hands as the sun came up, bringing a rich, overcoloured light to us on this our day. Out of the sun itself, it seemed, a line of saffron clad monks came in barefoot silence down the road. As each approached us, he removed the cover of his bowl and we placed our gifts in one by one. Each murmured a prayer over us and went quietly on his way.

After they had passed us by we sat long, holding hands, strangely moved and cleansed by the act of merit making we had performed. This is the only religious part of a Buddhist wedding in Thailand. We were now free until nine minutes past two when we would be married in accordance with the laws of the country. Pan busied himself with final arrangements for the grand reception. I rested for a few hours, had a quick light lunch and then with the help of Tip, Meow, Tari's hairdresser and the Gloria beauty supervisor, I was prepared like a goat for sacrifice. First I lay in Mae Khun's long white bath; hot water and bubbles; I had never before had a hot bath and I loved it. The hairdresser insisted on coming and washing my hair although I could perfectly well have done it myself; Mae Khun fussed around and Pim kept giving me sweets that I did not want and which I had to drop furtively into the lavatory. I sat on the big double bed while my hair was dried and my nails manicured and painted. Then I was lifted into a chair and the two girls began to work on my hair and face. When they had finished with me I feared Pan would think that the wrong girl had come to him, although I did not think he would, care, for she did look rather lovely.

I asked Tip to fetch my *pasin* and blouse, but instead she came back with a billowing mass of white silk and lace carried by yet another girl. This was Mae Khun's own wedding gown and the dressmaker deftly made some small alterations, tut-tutting through a mouthful of pins. Por Khun carried me down the stairs. I looked up at him, caught hold of his finger and lifted up his hand, which quickly passed over the danger zone and touched my cheek; then he bent down and, to the consternation of the Gloria supervisor, kissed me full on the mouth. We laughed aloud and suddenly I felt supremely confident as he placed me in my chair. The supervisor rushed up to redo my mouth and ordered Por Khun to go upstairs immediately and wash the lipstick off his face.

On a sofa sat my parents, Pan's mother, the Mayor of Mae Taeng and the Registrar of marriages. In front of them sat Pan, resplendent in a dark suit and grey tie. Tip pushed me up to his right side, the Mayor greeted us and passed the register for Pan to sign; just at that moment the Registrar whispered in the Mayor's ear, and looked at me, quickly he took back the book. Had something gone wrong at the last moment ? Was Pan already married ? I had heard of such things. I was on the wrong side, the bride should sit on the left. Among general laughter, we changed places. The book was signed. We were given our marriage certificates. We were man and wife.

Next came the *rot nam*, or water pouring ceremony. The Governor of Chiang Mai had agreed to preside over our wedding and it was he who, after we had prayed briefly at the altar set up to one side of the room, placed perfumed powder on our foreheads and put floral *lai* around our necks, beautiful *lai* that had been made in the Inner Palace where the last relatives of the consorts of previous kings still live in seclusion and where no man may enter. Next wreaths of cotton were placed on our heads, wreaths made from one thread so that they were joined together like us, for ever. Behind us stood my bridesmaids, Tip and Nongnai and Pan's best men Chand and a friend who was blind.

Our parents, relatives, friends and guests unknown to me, came before us one by one and murmuring words of good luck poured, from a conch shell, drops of lustral water, first onto my hands and then on to Pan's, as we held them out, palms pressed together. It was a moving ceremony, if tiring on the hands, and all the blessings we received that day would ensure, I felt certain, that we would always keep faith with each other, for so much goodwill could not lightly be cast away.

We rested awhile before the reception that was to be held on the lawn at five o'clock. Many more people came than had blessed us in the afternoon for this was a well planned public relations event to show that disabled people can lead a useful and happy life and be married like anyone else. The party was also intended to promote the Bua Geow Charity. Pun, Nongnai and some of the other girls sat working on a stage, and beside them sat four hilltribe girls, the originals of the four styles we made; Yao, Lisu, Akha and Meo, they looked splendidly exotic in their full tribal costumes.

We sat, Pan and I, in the house and greeted all the guests as they passed through. Some we knew, but many we did not. They wrote their names in our book and the bridesmaids gave each a small, cross-stitch bag with our names and the date embroidered on it. There was a television crew, reporters from newspapers and magazines, some important officials, several people in wheelchairs and, of course, the whole of our village who clustered together at the far end of the lawn looking rather bewildered and uncomfortable. We were just going outside to join the party when in swept the beautiful Tari followed by her encourage of handsome men. I do not know if her entrance had been planned, but it was perfectly timed. There was a hush and all heads turned as she bent to embrace me, then she did a funny thing, she stepped back and placed her hand on my forehead, as if blessing me; every camera flashed and the television spotlights blinded me. She was perfect that evening. She spoke to Chand, spent a long time with the village group and then went across to Pun, took her work from her and completed the hilltribe figure that Pun had been making; she then stuck it in a card, wrote something and presented it to a pleased governor. She said a few words that made him laugh, raised her left eyebrow and made a low *wai*.

Then it was time to cut the cake, a great seven-tiered wonder of white, standing in the middle of the buffet table. Pan picked up the knife and I playfully struggled with him, trying to place my hand on top of his. The pieces of cake were passed round to the guests and it was time for speeches and toasts. I refused either to speak or to taste the champagne, but Pan spoke so well, he talked of us and our plans, of how the body was of no great importance if your mind and spirit were strong. It was a message of hope and I was very proud of my husband.

At last all the guests left except for our parents, the old former *puyai baan* and his wife and a few close friends. We sat around tired, content and hardly talking. We still had to wait until nine minutes past ten o'clock for the putting-to-bed ceremony. I argued that, in our case, it was rather silly since we had already decided that we would not try to consumate our marriage, but Father insisted that everything must be done correctly and that the time given by Luang Por must be observed. The old *puyai baan* who had retired many years ago, had been asked by father to perform this final ceremony of the day, since his marriage had been so fruitful and happy. The time came near and we went into the room that had been prepared for us. The old couple placed a stone and a pumpkin under the bed, then they lay down on it and wished us as long a life, as many children, and as much happiness as they had had. It was nine minutes past the hour. Everyone blessed us and stole from the room leaving the girl in the looking-glass alone with her man.

90

We went to Mae Taeng the next day, it was Songkram. Tip made us get out of the car at Nongnai's house where an arch of bamboo, decorated with banana leaves had been placed across the lane. They had cut branches of scarlet flowered flame-tree and with them lined the way to our house. As we wheeled along all our friends threw jasmine scented water at us, the traditional northern way of greeting friends on this New Year's day; we were soon soaked to the skin. Outside our door we were touched to see the message "Welcome home Bua Geow and Pan" written with rose petals on the ground. We learned that it was Meow who had written this sweet greeting.

We settled easily into the rhythm of our new life together and there were few disagreements between us, even though Pan did not come from a farming background and found some of our family's ways rather strange. For me it is wonderful to be able to talk to someone about things other then garlic and village gossip. We spent hours making plans for the Bua Geow Charity, for Pan had agreed that we would take over its management. We would now have to buy the cards, envelopes and cloth, decide which figures should be made, how many and by whom, send out the orders, collect the money and keep the accounts. A group of Trustees in Chiang Mai would check the books and decide how any profit should be spent, although ideas of ours on how to spend the money would be very welcome.

So we made plans and dreamed. We would found a village where the disabled could live together as one large family, we would publish a magazine of our own. One day, as Pan was admiring me while I sat topless, brushing my hair, we decided to found a Mermaid Society and to hold beauty contests for those who could not walk. My parents thought us rather mad, and perhaps we were in our new-found happiness.

Meow's grandmother died soon after we were married. She slipped away, unmourned except by Meow, who came to live with us; she quickly took over all the tasks we could not do ourselves; she it was who went to Chiang Mai to buy materials and deliver cards, who posted the parcels and distributed cloth and thread to the other girls. She looked after the house, did the washing, and all the other things that we could not do ourselves. She and Luk Nam became to us the children that we would never have.

In June Chand entered the monkhood. It is the custom in Thailand for almost all men to become a monk for a period of time, maybe for a week or a month; most often for the three months of the rainy season Buddhist Lent, sometimes for ever. Formerly a family would give at least one of their sons to the *wat* as a child where he would be educated and where he usually spent the rest of his life. Nowadays families are smaller, there are government schools and many attractions for a boy in the big towns. When a boy becomes a novice there is a great celebration. His parents, or if they can not afford it, an elder person in the village, will buy his robes. Painted and dressed up, often as a girl, he is led in procession by the whole village to the *wat* riding, maybe, on a horse surrounded with dancers and musicians. He is received by the Abbot, his head and eyebrows are shaved by his mother, his fancy clothes taken away and replaced with saffron robes which may be his garb for ever.

We took Chand to the *wat* dressed in a white robe, mother shaved his head, father gave him his robes, begging bowl, bag, spoon and fork, and Pra Noi led him away to change into his saffron robes and to start his new life of self-denial and meditation. Mother is so happy, for if a son becomes a monk before he marries, all the merit from his act accrues to his mother, after marriage it goes to his wife. We girls still believe that a boy who has never been ordained is unripe and spiritually not ready for marriage.

Chand has not said how long he plans to remain at the *wat* and of course he can come out anytime he likes and resume his ordinary life; I hope this will be before the fields need to be ploughed. We see him in the early morning as he walks past with his alms bowl and it gives mother enormous pleasure to bow down before him, or before his robe, as she places food in his bowl. He does not raise his eyes to her.

Pun's house is finished and they moved in today. It is very well built, the roof of tiles, the wall brick as far as the window, wood above, the floor cement; there is a bedroom, a kitchen and a lavatory and in front one large space that serves as shop and living area. Pan and I went round the village and collected small donations from people, things that she can stock her shop with, when first she opens. Our Charity has spent Bts. 27,000 on the house and has also bought her stock to the value of Bts. 3,000 – packets of detergent, soap, candles, sanitary towels, sweets, medicine and so on. Pun and Geow looked so pleased with themselves as they sat on the floor surrounded by boxes and packets. I asked if I could be their first customer and bought some sweets which I passed to the children who peeked through the windows. Here I think is another story with a happy ending.

At first I did not know who she was, a rather frail girl walking through the gate, then old memories flooded back. She was Ying, Chand's first girlfriend, the *puyai baan's* daughter. She told us that, after her father had rejected Chand's proposal, he had found a much more suitable match in the form of a junior government official who worked for the Land Department. She was not consulted in the matter and was sent with unseemly haste to live with her new husband at his parent's house in Mae Rim. Ying hated her mother-in-law from the very first day; she controlled every action of her darling boy, watching over him and ordering him about as if he was still in the nursery. When alone, they got on tolerably well together, but he would hear no word of criticism against his mother. In any argument he always sided with his mother and, no matter how rudely and harshly Ying was treated, he never once supported her.

When the final explosion came, it was over some insignificant point but three years of bottled up frustration and anger burst out of Ying. She threw a bucket of dirty water at her mother-in-law, slapped her husband and walked out of the house. When she reached home her father was furious and shut her up in her room, but even though none of her family would now speak to her, nothing, she said, would ever persuade her to go back to her husband.

The first thing I did was to give her some material, thread and a needle; I had come to think of our work as a kind of therapy that distracted people's thoughts from their troubles and brought them peace and pleasure; I had seen it succeed with Pun, Meow and myself. The second thing I did was send word to Chand in his solitary cell; I knew I sinned by disturbing his meditation with visions of a former love, but I am a born match-maker and I could already imagine them married and living with their children in our compound, for Ying had nowhere else to go.

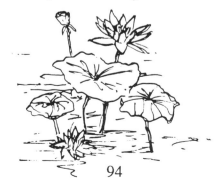

94

Pan had borrowed a pile of books on farming and for days he had been reading through them making notes in the last of my yellow school books; he has not told me much about his studies, but this evening he began to talk to father and Chand. I was intensely proud of his new-found knowledge. He came up with suggestions and ideas supported with facts and figures. Did father know that on a cost per *rai* calculation garlic was one of the worst crops to grow, that strawberries were better by a factor of four and potatoes by a factor of three ? If I could, I would have kicked him under the table, for behind the polite 'yeses' from father and Chand I could see a wall of disbelief and suspicion going up, just as it did when agricultural experts came to the village, and I must confess Pan sounded rather like one of them.

As soon as I could I called him outside and explained gently that it would take years of patient repetition and persuasion before he could change father's ideas and I suggested that he should not even try yet. Crestfallen he agreed that I was problaby right and we began to talk of our planned magazine, our Charity and the Mermaid Society. Pan returned the books he had borrowed and we settled again into the rythm of village life together.

Chand left the monkhood sooner than anyone had expected until they heard of his engagement to Ying.

We hear sensational gossip about Tari as the date of the Miss Thailand contest draws near and she is tipped to be the first Miss Chiang Mai ever to win. Tari or Tammatari, as she is now always called, has become quite a Chamadevi cult figure with a deep interest in family and house spirits which I am sure is good for tourism. She is also a leading light in the Women's Liberation League.

The rains came early this year and father has been worrying that the rice would suffer, but, for the past three days it has not rained at all; I have been able to go outside with Pan and the mountains have been quite clear.

END NOTES

The article on ceramics originally appeared in The Journal of the Siam Society.

The notes on Bhuddism were given to Chand when he was in the monkhood.

The account of Tari and her 'honey' has been compiled from various scurrilous articles in the local gutter press.

Notes on Ceramics

In September thousands of ceramic wares appeared in the antique shops of Bangkok, Sukhothai and Chiang Mai. There were beautiful large 14th century Chinese celadons, Ming blue and white wares, spectacular underglaze black decorated dishes and bowls from Sukhothai-town and Sawankaloke, celadons from Sawankaloke, Kalong-Wang Nua and San Kamphaeng, superb late Haripunchai water bottles and an extraordinary and quite unknown group of white wares, some with vivid inglaze green decoration which many now believe to have been made in the area of Pegu in Burma.

The wildest stories circulated. This was booty being taken back to Burma after the sack of Ayutthaya in 1569 or was it 1767 ? They must have been dead soldiers, as swords were so often found in the graves, soldiers presumably fighting with plates, bowls and their very own burial urn in their knapsacks. Or were the goods from a series of markets along the old trade route to Martaban, the great port of Burma. Perhaps they were burial sites but if so whose, high up in the mountains ?

The only fact clearly established was that these artifacts were indeed coming from the Mae Sot area of Tak Province near the Burmese border.

Then in February another deluge of ceramics surged into the antique market, this time from the Mae Tun-Omkoi area further north, in Chiang Mai Province. Here there were many more wares from Lan Na, mostly from San Kamphaeng and now including some underglaze black decorate dishes, but also superb Kalong monochromes and black and white pieces, Phan and Phayao wares and large brown glazed jars from no known kiln.

It is now definite that all these ceramics came from hilltop burial sites. Thousands of graves from at least forty sites have already been looted; they are scattered throughout the mountain spine of Thailand, from Omkoi and Mae Tun in the north, down through Mae Ramat and Ban Tak, Tak and Mae Sot, to Kamphaeng Phet and Umphang, and there is a strong probability that they extend much further north and south and also well into Burma. In almost all cases the sites are too far away from the main lowland valleys, where it is thought that wet-rice cultivating Thais lived, for it to be conceivable that it was they who carried the ashes of their dead unto the mountains for burial. Nor are the sites, with one or two exceptions, near any likely major trade routes although local trade routes undoubtedly followed the mountain ridges. The probability that these wares are in any way connected with international trade routes is remote in any case since they are so totally different from the selection of ceramics found in Indonesia, the Middle East or India, which would seem to be the most likely markets for goods shipped from Martaban. The wares from Sukhothai must have passed through Ayutthaya, which controlled the export trade, before going on to Indonesia and the Philippines, the two great markets for Sukhothai ceramics.

A few graves are reported to contain skeletons but with the exception of one lowland site at Mae Taeng* the vast majority contain either ashes and small bones in a jar, or else there is no remaining trace of any ashes at all. It seems therfore that the body was usually first cremated and the ashed then buried with grave furniture.

---

*   *This particular site is not typical and although it contains some artifacts from this period it may well be dateable to the late seventeenth century.*

The grave sites are occasionally marked with a menhir; in other places depressed circles of varying size are clearly visible circumscribing areas which contain one or more graves.

The burial sites do not seem to predate 1300 and only very few pieces that could conceivable be given a Sung (960–1276) date are known. The difficulty of differentiating between Sung, Yuan and early Ming celadons, especially provincial export wares, is notorious. All we can say is that the Tak sites have the appearance of being 14th century – 16th century. Many wares seems to be late 14th century – the Chekiang celadons, the early blue and white wares and, by association, many of the Sukhothai and Lan Na wares. The ubiquitous blue and white bowls could be dated as late as the middle of the 16th century but there appears to be nothing with a post-Ming (1368-1644) date. It therefore seems likely that the inhabitants of this mountainous no man's land that divided the kingdoms of Burma from those of Thailand flourished during the Golden Age of early Ayuthaya and Lan Na perhaps from the middle of the 14th century, coinciding with the founding of Ayuthaya in 1351, until the devastation of Thailand by the Burmese in the middle of the 16th century.

We do not known who these mountain people were who so lovingly buried their dead with ceramics of value and with other personal possessions such as bronze lime-pots, bracelets, bells and mirrors, iron swords, knives, axes and daggers, beads of rock crystal and coloured glass and sometimes with gold. But always with ceramics – for the rich, an elephant urn or superb Sukhothai, Chinese or Kalong wares; for others, less fine wares from China, Sukhothai, Lan Na, Burma and Vietnam, and for the poorest, what are probably locally made coarse earthenwares.

Who were these people ? Were they perhaps the Lawa, the original inhabitants of north Thailand, about whom so little is known and if so did they barter forest products, which were so important in the Chinese tribute trade, for these lovely ceramics carrying them down the mountain tracks to local markets at the frontiers of Lan Na or Ayuthaya, or perhaps even to the great trade centres of Tak, Chiang Mai or Pitsanuloke ?

A Fragment on Bhuddhism Give To Me
by Phra Chand

A Buddhist is someone who has declared his faith and interest in finding out more about the Triple Gem which is to say: The Lord Buddha, The *Dhamma,* or the Way that he taught and which can lead to Enlightenment and *Nirvana,* and the Noble Order of Enlightened followers, the *Sangha* or monks that we see today.

Having declared ones faith three times in the ancient Pali language to a monk, he will then chant and ask you to repeat the Five Precepts.

I promise that I will start training myself not to destroy life.

I promise that I will start training myself not to take anything that has not been freely given to me.

I promise that I will start training myself to refrain from wrong-doing in sexual desire.

I promise that I will start training myself not to tell lies or speak badly or loosely.

I promise that I will start training myself not to take distilled or fermented intoxicants which can lead me into trouble.

The monk then says: "Guard these three Jewels and Five Precepts well, they are for your own good and you must make a conscious effort to follow them."

You have now taken the first step along the way to Enlightenment.

But you will certainly need a good Teacher to help you, particularly if you are to make progress towards Concentration, Wisdom and Meditation.

The way in which these precepts are worded immediately shows up the great difference between Buddhism and most of the other major religions with their God given Commandments "Thou shalt not......."

Gautama was born near the Indian–Nepal border some 560 years before Jesus. The fifth and sixth centuries before Christ produced a great effervescence of religious and philosophical thought throughout the known world. In the advanced civilisation of the Ganges basin both the Buddha and Jain Mahavira led movements against the cast system and against the sacrifices of the Brahmans. Both believed in rebirth and showed how to escape from its endless progression. Jainism remains a small sect in India whereas Buddhism lost its hold in the country of its birth and became a world religion.

This too was the period of Zoroaster which produced the Parsi sect. It was also the period of the Hebrew Prophets of Lao Tzo and Confucious in China and of the philosophical schools of Pythagorus and Socrates.

Guatama was born to a rich, if not princely, family, was brought up in a sheltered life of luxury, married and had a son. Then one day He was shocked to discover the suffering of human life, the pain, anxiety and death. He abandoned everything and sought, through consulting sages and practicing asceticism, a solution to the problem. Finally through His own efforts and because He already was Bodhisatta He was able to achieve Enlightenment, and with it complete knowledge so that His wisdom enabled Him to see the total truth of everything. All His past lives He saw; He knew exactly how everyone's past actions effected their present ones and how their present ones would shape their future. He saw to the root causes of all the unsatisfactoriness of life (Dukka), the desire for pleasure, the desire to continue life. and the great problem of ignorance which

103

prevents people from seeing the truth and doing the right things.

When He stood up in the morning He was the The Lord Buddha and in His great pity for the suffering of mankind He resolved to pass on His discovery to all those who would listen. And this He did for the next forty years, preaching throughout the Ganges Valley.

In almost all religions you have to make that great leap in the dark to accept in faith. In Buddhism, you can proceed along the way as far as you are able knowing that in your next life you have the chance to progress further. The Lord Buddha taught in different ways to different people according to their own level of understanding and He told them not to accept anything blindly until they had worked it out for themselves. Thus some serious Buddhist disciples scale the north face of the mountain in an attempt to reach Nirvana in their present life, but most laymen meander peacefully along the gentle paths of the foothills.

The secret of contentment is within yourself and those who practice mediation go far along the path and achieve much peace of mind in this stressful age. They do not need to, and should not, worry about abstruse points of religious theory.

And some questions by P.

And so the days crawled by – meditation chanting, and long, heated arguments with the *acharn*: though these were more like debates than arguments since I had a lot of questions about Buddhism and religion in general and I felt that these nuns should be able to answer them. Most of the people attending were shocked by my audacity but I explained that the Buddha taught that we should never believe without reason, and I wanted to know the reasons why I should believe. The fact that I'm a rather firm atheist

104

didn't go down well with the nuns either. The *acharn* was a different matter; modern, not easily shocked, so that she seemed to enjoy dealing with me. But how disappointing it was to find that no one could satisfactorily anwer the questions I was putting to them – like, 'Does one get more merit by donating millions to build golden pagodas than by saving the environment? If so, why? If not, how can we explain that Thai temples are one of the richest institutions in the country? Then again, what right did the Buddha have in a former life to give away his wife and children to a man who was a proven scoundrel? And as the Buddha never put into exact words what rebirth, nirvana and so on are, how come we've been so presumptious as to do it for ourselves? Etc...etc...etc.

The answer I got to all these questions and more was, I can't explain it to you, but if you mediate, you'll find it out for yourself.

Tari and Her Honey

Tari has done well by her husband. The three years she had invested in him had yielded an excellent return. Not that she would, for one moment, have thought of her marriage in so calculating and cynical a light for she had truly cared for, and respected, her husband. But love ? No, and of that she was as good a judge as any.

Her husband had been, and still was, a highly respected and extremely successful banker. Rich Chinese business-men, even when thirty years older, have much to offer a young girl with no background or education, even if she happens to be, as Tari was, Miss Thailand and a Miss Universe finalist. Let me hasten to add that what such men have to offer is not only sordid money, useful though that may prove to be, for many of them are distinguished and courteous gentlemen who well know how to use their experienced, if elderly, charm. So it was that he had swooped her up to the chagrin of more than one highly eligible young suitor who had dallied too long and concentrated, perhaps not enough, on this one single object of desire.

After three years she had successfully consolidated her position. He had set her up in business of her own. This was a beauty salon, called Tari Thai, which occupied the ground floor of two adjoining town houses in a quiet *soi* off Sukumvit Road. Above was a very comfortable flat where she now lived, for she had found out that her husband had made similar arrangements with at least four other girls, the only difference was that he had never married them, although he supported and frequently visited these, his *mia noi*.

Tari, however, was his *mia luang*, his legal wife, and she would not tolerate such a diversity of interests now that

106

it had become generally known to her friends and now that she was financially secure. Once she had checked with her lawyer that the title-deeds of the town-houses and control of the company were securely in her name, she demanded a divorce. No doubt surprised, her husband was not entirely dismayed and the separation was arranged to the satisfaction of both parties.

With a twinge of conscience she realised that she had not been the best of wives. She had produced no son, not even a daughter, and she had, after the first few weeks, seldom been with her husband except when she wished him to escort her to grand functions. She spent more and more time with her own group of friends, just as he did with his. Both had benefited from the marriage. She had made herself financially secure and independent for life and, even more important, she had learned much from him about banking and business. He had increased his prestige no end by winning such a coveted prize – the losing of it did not matter for the possession was on record.

We see her now reclining on a pile of silk cushions on the floor of her sitting-room. On the table beside her are a glass of passion fruit juice and a bowl of sliced mango that her maid has just placed there. She is reading the gossip column of Thai Rath, no doubt to see if her name is mentioned, for on the previous day she had attended a reception at the Oriental Hotel for a visiting American Senator. It is ten o'clock in the morning and she is still in her diaphanous pink night-dress, but it is, after all, Sunday and she came home late last night, so we need not criticise her. Normally she is always in her office by eight o'clock.

Even though she wears no make-up and has not even washed the sleep from her eyes, she is dramatically beautiful. Long legs stretched out, black hair falling around her creamy shoulders, a few unruly wisps straying across her forehead as if leading the way to those devastating dark eyes which look so innocent and helpless but which have caused so many a promise of fidelity to be broken. Perhaps she is not so slender as she had been when she won her title but, in the opinion of many connoisseurs, she is all the better for that.

The room is tastefully furnished, and one must suspect the hand of a professional interior decorator for nothing seems to reveal her personality except for the wall of photographs. Photographs of herself as Miss Thailand, as a finalist in Caracas, and standing smiling with the famous and the rich. Balanced on a table in one corner are the tall, garishly vulgar trophies of her calling.

Let us lean over her delectable shoulder for a few minutes as she lazily looks through the scrap-book of her life which she has now picked up from the table beside her. Her history and her memory conveniently start when she won the Miss Chiang Mai contest. Few would now believe that she had been born to a poor illiterate farmer in the obscure village of Mae Tang where she had toiled, bent and burned, in fields of rice and garlic. Again we must be fair to her for it had been her image builders who so entirely expunged her early life from the record. Successful contestants had to be sophisticated and intelligent, brains were as important as beauty, they said, in deference to the feminist movements and so another childhood was created for her. The earliest entry in the scrap-book, therefore, is a photograph of her sitting gloriously atop her float in the Chiang Mai floral procession.

We turn page after page of receptions and Gloria Cosmetic promotions, for this company had been her sponsor, in the weeks that led up to, and followed after, her crowning as Miss Thailand. She had worked very hard and with remarkable success to prepare herself for the competition which no Miss Chiang Mai had ever won. She planned even more carefully her assault on the Miss Universe peak. She attended a deportment school and then went to Penang where she was assiduous in her study of English even, perhaps, falling a little in love with her tutor, her first, but no means her last, foreign conquest.

She arrived in Caracas with high hopes accompanied by Ajarn who was the owner of Gloria Cosmetics and a suitably steady chaperone. She endeared herself to the press corps, won the Miss Photogenic title and sailed confidently into the finals. But it was not to be for politics, as well as favours given or promised, come into play in the final selection, and politics she could not control. Unfortunately for Tari, Asia had recently overreached itself. In the past ten years the Philippines had won twice and there was, of course, Thailand's own Apasara. A further winner from the region would not be acceptable and so it was on the beautiful golden head of Miss Iceland that the crown was placed.

Tari was not too greatly upset. Ajarn left for Bangkok the day after the contest, furious that she had not won, for victory would, he calculated, have increased his sales by forty percent, but even more furious because she had abandoned him for others. The chaperone faithfully followed Tari wherever she went giving a great impression of respectability without, in fact, limiting her activities in any way.

The six months she spent in the Americans and Europe turned a brash little country girl on the make into a highly sophisticated lady of the world. She passed through the care of some of the wealthiest and most brilliant members of the international set and no one could have received better grooming in the ways of the world. Her quick intelligence enabled her to pick up much more than just a veneer of cosmopolitan elegance, she actually became one of the accepted members of this glittering group.

In the privileged seventeenth century she would have been a mistress of Louis XIV or Charles II, now in our democratic era, she spread her favours more evenly. A less complete personality, someone with education and a middle class background, would have been irredeemably spoiled if not destroyed by so sudden a rise to such a life. But her very lack of education and background, her peasant sense, enabled her to stand outside herself, as it were, and thoroughly enjoy the spectacle of it all without being, in her true and inner self, violated. Yes, she slept with many a suave man of celebrity and not a few elderly bloods of family, but she emerged from this finishing school greatly enriched and as pure and innocent as on the day she left her home. And this was no small achievement. I am reminded of an old Cornish miracle play in which it was written. "As the sun goes through glass without breaking it so Christ above went into Mary's womb without defiling any joint."

She returned to Bangkok and took her place in society as if to the manner born. If it was a frivolous and useless life, there were many with far less excuse than Tari who spent their days in the desire and pursuit of pleasure. There was about her at this time, as a few of her more discerning friends noticed, a waiting air; as a lonely wife will sit late at night with her head slightly tilted listening for the sound of a key in the door.

As she sticks the report of yesterday's reception into her scrap-book we will quietly leave her, but as we turn away I notice that she has carelessly left the bedroom door open, so let us take this chance to enter, even though it may not be the last time that we shall do so. The room is surprisingly spartan, the colour scheme black and white, and there are no trophies or photographs. The dressing table is, naturally, littered with the pots, tubes and jars of her profession and the jewellery box, which lies open, is ablaze with dazzling stones, for she had never found it in her heart to wound her friends by refusing the proffered tokens of their admiration.

Open on the floor is her suitcase for this very day she is leaving for a holiday in England, to be precise, Oxford.

David Strangh slipped naturally into the routine of College life. He had taken up his appointment as Waynflete Professor of Asian History, joining that great school at Magdalen created and nurtured by K.B. McFarlane, A.J.P. Taylor, Karl Leyser and John Stoye, a school in which, so he once wrote, "High intellectual standards and an emphasis on self-discipline had been combined with, indeed fostered by, a libertarian and humane esprit de corps."

He took up residence in May and who, returning from long years in the tropics, could have failed to revel in the bursting joy of that spring. Each morning as he strolled from Hollywell Ford, down Addison's Walk, he thrilled to the sounds, the colours and the scents. He marvelled at the towering chestnuts with their pyramid white torches, the laburnums prodigally pouring gold on to the ground and the fritillaries with their heads darkly bowed before the buttercups in the Meadows. As he passed through the gates he would look first at the Tower on his left, rising in majesty above the cloisters, and then to the right over the velvet lawns where stretched the New Building fringed with dripping wisteria. Beyond lay the Grove with its crop of summer dappled deer. This was the very heart of England. He belonged here and all this now belonged to him.

David Strangh was not old, he had in fact been born while the Battle of Britain raged overhead and now, five years after his arrival at Oxford, he was nearing the age of forty-six and he had never felt more physically and mentally alive. He was wont to say that men reached their over-all prime at that age – had not both Wellington and Napoleon been forty-six at the battle of Waterloo ?

He was, it is true, going somewhat bald, but that only tended to accentuate the high reach of his unlined forehead which seemed to rest comfortably on the wheels of his glasses. Any bare patch there may have been further back was well concealed by a luxuriant growth of grey hair which was allowed to blow unkempt over his collar and ears in academic abandon. His face was cheerfully rubicund, either from long years under the tropical sun, or, perhaps, from a slight predilection for, in Thailand, Singha beer and Mekong and, at Oxford, claret and port, for the famous Magdalen cellars yielded a never ending supply of excellent vintages.

He was conservative in his dress, not to say out-of-date and eccentric. In the cooler months he wore coarsely woven tweed suits – green and brown were his favourite colours – with a matching waistcoat straining against the thrust of a happy paunch. Across it, from pocket to pocket, as if in further precaution against expansion, stretched a gold chain to which was attached a signed Julien Le Roy quarter repeater bearing the date 1740 on the ring of the dial. This beautifully balanced watch, he liked to say, had originally been exported to China whence it found its way via the Thieves Market of Bangkok into his pocket.

In summer he invariably wore a fawn coloured light-weight tropical jacket with grey trousers – except on Saturdays when he sported white flannels. The ties he wore were handwoven in Lavenham except again on Saturdays when they were O.S. or R.B.S.C. His one idiosyncrasy lay in his choice of brightly coloured socks – they never, even by chance, seemed to match the rest of his carefully modulated colour scheme, or even, at times, each other.

This, then, was the man who stood on the lawns of Magdalen one magnificent May morning, a man who had found his place in life and intended to enjoy it for many years to come. It had not been easy for him to achieve his ambition and become an Oxford don. For long it had seemed an impossible dream, for his lacadaisical approach to history when an undergraduate had resulted in a totally undistinguished second. It was only his impressive and meticulous work in the entirely uncharted field of English intercourse with Siam in the late Seventeenth Century and the fortuitious creation of a Professorship in Asian History that had brought him back to his college.

He fulfilled his role brilliantly and five years of profitable happiness followed. As a tutor he stirred interest in several unexpected quarters. As a lecturer his knowledge and enthusiasm caught the imagination of many, some right outside historical circles, and his room at Schools on Tuesdays and Thursdays was always full. This was a period, too, of mature and fruitful publication on Siamese Seventeenth Century administrative reforms that received favourable notice well beyond the frontiers of Oxford.

He and his wife entertained students, fellows and friends at delightfully informal yet stimulating dinner parties and his theories on the way in which the unfolding of history should be traced by the study, not of famous men or economic factors, but rather by such social phenomena as corruption, patronage, elites and servants, brought him an unusual group of followers. He held, too, that the study of these matters, and, indeed, of the people as a whole in Asian countries such as Thailand, would give European historians an entirely new perspective on the field of their research. Peasant farmers, seignoral prerogatives, electoral malpractices, nepotism and monopolies, Victorian attitudes to poverty and prostitution, all these and more were at a stage of development in Asia that they had long since passed through in Europe.

He joined, too, in the life of his college, Not an athlete, he could be seen every morning striding in a rolling fashion round the Walks and in the summer he played a weekly game of tennis with the Bursar. His main hobby was the study of college history in, naturally enough, the

114

Seventeenth Century. He was saddened that he could not discover any member of Magdalen or of Oxford who had visited Siam during his period. He enjoyed the thought that King Charles I, attended by Prince Rupert, had watched the threatening movement of Essex's troops from the Tower in 1644. He drew maps of the defences that were thrown up in the Walks at Dover Pier and elsewhere. He became engrossed in the famous confrontation between the Fellows and King James II in 1687-8 that resulted in the expulsion of twenty-five Fellows about whom he wrote. "They may justly be allowed the honour which is due to those who are willing to abide, be the cost what it may, by the rules of duty and conscience".

Then Tari arrived and he blew it all.

It was, we all agreed afterwards, for the subject was frequently discussed in the Senior Common Room, very bad luck.

Tari had been invited to stay by the Thai wife of a close friend of David's, a Fellow of Merton. It was therefore natural that he should meet her for dinner on the day of her arrival, the more so since he had been introduced to her in Chiang Mai after she had won her title, not, he was certain, that she would remember.

As usual David's wife was away, this time attending a three month meditation course. As he so often said forty-six is an important age for a man. It is also a dangerous one, for youth is now firmly behind and old age looms ahead.

This is the age when highly revered pillars of society fall in love with their secretaries and desert their families. Although David respected his wife and enjoyed her company when she happened to be at home, love had, for many years, played no part in their relationship. For long they had slept in separate rooms. However his strict moral code made it unthinkable that he should be unfaithful, or so he, and we, firmly believed. Yet in truth he was vulnerable and doubled.

His relations with female students were stiffly correct. He did not disapprove of them like a certain professor who, in the early days of female penetration into Oxford, removed his trousers in the lecture hall – only when all the girl undergraduates had duly departed did he draw them on again and continue with his discourse. Nor was Strangh the avuncular type who would make much use of his hands to demonstrate a point and encourage girls to come for extra tuition in his rooms. Never had there been a whisper of scandal and the college wives ever on the alert, were, perforce, silent.

116

Then Tari arrived.

It was a large and formal gathering that evening for it happened to be the fiftieth birthday of Tari's host. David was standing at the far end of the long room, his glass resting on the grand-piano, conspicuous in his cummerbund which he often wore to emphasise his oriental connections. Tari was late. She swept into the room and paused, poised in the doorway. For a second it was as if the film of all that was happening had stopped. There was a sudden stillness as heads turned and conversations trailed away unfinished and unattended. Good breeding soon covered this hiccup of bad manners and the renewed noise of voices rose in decibels.

She stood there smiling, waiting for her hosts, beautiful and exotic.

She wore a shimmering dark green sheath dress of Thai silk with no sleeves and a plunging neck-line where, in a slight depression, nestled a green coloured elephant. David, who had stood transfixed, now strode rapidly across the room and introduced himself.

"You will not remember me but we met in Chiang Mai on the day you won your crown."

"But I do remember, You were at Ajarn's party where we all drank champagne and poor Bua Geow went bright red and passed out. Of course I remember you, David", she laughed.

She came close and they shook hands. She held his hand for a long time looking quizzically into his eyes, her thumb pressed gently, twice, on the back of his hand sending shock waves tingling through his heart. From that moment he was lost, for Tari had arrived.

She had remembered him! He monopolised her all evening for they had many mutual friends and they could talk together in Thai even, to her delight, in *Kam Muang,*

117

the northern dialect of her youth. They sat next to each other at dinner and he completely ignored the wife of the Dean of Divinity who sat on his right. This affront started the gossip that soon rose to such pitch that it broke, so some said, the stained glass window in the Chapel.

He left the party, intoxicated, even though he had drunk much less than usual. They had arranged to meet next day for lunch at the Randolph, and so they did. Afterwards they strolled back to Magdalen; past Martyr's Memorial, and down The Broad, they went: beyond Balliol and Trinity, David suddenly stopped in front of Blackwell's and stared at the weathered Emperors standing before the Sheldonian. Long he looked but no great beads of perspiration glistered on their brows. Once, thus had they warned, in vain, against the presence of Zuleika Dobson. Now they took no notice of Tari. Perhaps they could not fathom her eastern powers, perhaps they were not concerned with the nemesis of one middle-aged don – or perhaps they secretly envied him his fate.

They wandered round the college grounds, and then had tea in his rooms – Earl Grey accompanied by anchovies on toast and chocolate cake. He talked of his research and showed her old Thai manuscripts that she could not read. In everything Tari was greatly interested, punctuating his lecture with exclamations of wonder and surprise, leading him on with intelligent comments and questions.

By the time they walked back to Merton, hand-in-hand, that luminous evening, he was in love with the infatuated intensity of the middle-aged.

It was not that Tari had set out to capture David. Why should she ? A dull don was no great prize for one who had dined at the tables of Princes and drunk from the barrels of oil tycoons. But she was, it must be admitted, attracted to older men – she had, in fact, virtually no experience with those of her own age whom she found impetuous and lacking in worship. She took an almost erotic pleasure in stripping away the dusty, crusty layers that surrounded a successful man, to reveal the boy whom she almost always found lurking somewhere within. A boy who had never grown up, and never would, in spite of the coating of pomposity, composed of money, fame and lust, stuck together with the glue of pretence, that had grown around him.

She had played the game so often that instinctively she could press – or undo –the right button causing yet another sector of her victim's defence to crumble. After all this time, her so-easily-won victories never failed to send a shiver of delight and excitement through her body just as when she stood on the edge of a high cliff.

David had been caught from the very first moment of their introduction when she had said that she remembered him so clearly. In fact she could not remember him at all but when her hostess had written inviting her to come to Oxford, she had mentioned that their friend, David Strangh, had met Tari the day she become Miss Chiang Mai. Tari always did her homework well and much of her social success was due to this. Now she looked through her scrap-book until she found the old faded photographs of the party given by Ajarn after she had won her title. Only one *farang* apart from Por Khun had been there. The rest was easy.

Tari found David refreshingly different and therefore interesting. Most of her acquaintances were men of the world, sophisticated and experienced. David was incredibly naive, especially as far as women were concerned. So every day in that glorious week of May they were together. They behaved like undergraduates. They walked up the High holding hands; they spent hours sight-seeing or shopping; they went for picnics; punted in the twilight under the trees of the Cherwell and danced close together at dimly lit parties. They were not aware of the crescendo of gossip, they were only aware of each other, for they were in love.

Yes, Tari, too was in love. She found it hard to believe as she stared in disapproval at her lovely face in the looking-glass her left eyebrow quizzically raised. Naturally he had fallen in love with her – how could he have avoided it? But what did she see in him? Certainly he was not hansome or distinguished – on the contrary. Under her gentle prodding he had, it is true, developed a surprising, dry, academic sense of humour made the more amusing for not always being intended. His jokes and stories about his colleagues were deliciously malicious. She enjoyed the small presents he gave her, each one of which had some hidden meaning or message that he explained to her (like the pink and black plastic earrings). Such valueless gifts would normally have been passed on to servants or relatives, but now she knew that she would treasure them. Oxford, seen with a knowlegeable and entertaining guide, had been a joy transcending her normal experience. But there was something else she could not define. Moth-like she was attracted to the light of an intellectual brilliance to which she had never before been exposed. Something inside her being was kindled and excited. She craved to know more about those subjects that David mentioned so casually. She felt too, that, more than anyone she had ever known, he needed to be looked after, protected and loved. This brought out emotions new to her. Perhaps for the first time in her life she was thinking of someone else – his needs and his pleasures – before herself and her own.

Radiating happiness and love she strolled in bliss and beauty through the heart of Oxford and many there were who sighed, some with sadness, some with relief, when she left. She caused cars to stall in the Corn, boats to bump on the Isis and many a swain to be rebuked as faithless by his mistress. One day she was seen to skip in the Turl and songs with this new rhythm were sung. Her eyes, like the sun, shone equally on all and crowds gathered wherever she went – even in Chapel. Tari hairstyles and Tari hats were all the fashion until the end of Hilary term. On one thing only all the men agreed: David was utterly unworthy of her. While to the college ladies Tari was of course a shameless hussy.

But the day came, when, as usual, the sun peered into Tari's bedroom and found it empty. She had caught, who knows with what emotions, the early train to London where she was attending a conference on beauty treatment of the mature, at which she had been asked to award the prizes.

David sank into a sullen mood of muddy dejection. The lectures that once had galvanised his audiences were now mumbled, perfunctory and boring as if he wished only to empty the hall as soon as possible so that he could return to brood in his rooms. He missed tutorials and snubbed his colleagues and worse, their wives.

Finally he was summoned by the President who told Strangh that although he could, perhaps, overlook his extraordinary behaviour during the visit of his Thai lady friend, he could not ignore his continuing dereliction of duty. In the discretely civilised way of Oxford the President suggested that he should take immediate sabbatical leave for one year.

I went to visit him in his rooms. Open on the floor was his suitcase, for on the next day he was leaving for Thailand; to be precise, Bangkok.